Bob HOPE

Bob HOPE

BY LEONARD PITTS JR.

A STARBOOK
Sharon Publications, Inc.
Cresskill, N.J. 07626

Bob Hope the man with the funny Ski nose.
An ambassador of good will—a humanitarian.
A man who gives generously, and tirelessly
donates his life on behalf of worthwhile causes.

The man who at great personal cost to himself,
dedicated his life to making people laugh.

This is a STARBOOK

All correspondence and inquiries should be directed to Sales Dept., Sharon
Publications, Inc., 105 Union Avenue, Cresskill, New Jersey 07626.
Sharon Publications, Inc. is an Edrei Communications Company.
ISBN #0-89531-077-5
Manufactured in the United States of America.

Editor: Mary J. Edrei
Cover and Book Design by Rod Gonzalez
Research Assistant: Cynthia Griffin

CHAPTER 1
THE EARLY YEARS
•
CHAPTER 2
BREAKING THROUGH
•
CHAPTER 3
THE WAR YEARS
•
CHAPTER 4
REFLECTIONS
•
CHAPTER 5
THE MOVIES

INTRODUCTION

The incredible Bob Hope! A master of monologue, the guy whose career started as half a dance act in a vaudeville show over sixty years ago.

Born Leslie Townes Hope on May 29th, 1903 in the London suburb of Eltham, he was not born into poverty, but poverty was soon thrust upon him. His father William Henry Hope, a stonemason by trade, found a demand for his services vanishing. After relocating his family twice, as he searched for work, he decided to make the big move—across the Atlantic to the United States . . .

So begins the life story of a man whom Presidents, heads of State and captains of Industry are honored to call a friend.

A man who has logged more miles than any other performer, to bring entertainment to "our boys" and to maintain the morale of the fighting men.

All those years in the limelight however, were not without great personal cost to him, for all the time spent away from his loved ones.

His amazing record! His durability, the honors bestowed on him—all make this compassionate man—a legend and an American Institution.

THE EARLY YEARS

CHAPTER 1 ●

IT WAS THE SUMMER of 1921. The eighteen-year-old youth was working in the wilds of the Cuyahoga Valley in Ohio for the Southern Ohio Power Company. He was at the top of a tall pine on this particular day, tying a tow rope, when the tree unexpectedly started to totter. Too much of its base had been sawed away.

The young man at the top held on for dear life as the tree swayed. And then the unthinkable happened: the tree fell. With only seconds to act, the youth scampered to the upper side of the tumbling trunk. That move saved his body, but when the tree crashed to the ground, there was no power on earth that could save his face. The impact of the fall crushed the young man's face against the wood and knocked him cold.

"I woke up in the hospital," he has said, "and they wouldn't give me a mirror for three weeks. I was worried, but I felt lucky to be alive. My family was relieved when they found out there were no brain injuries, but the doctors had to rearrange my nose and face."

That rearranging created a chin that juts almost cartoonishly and a long, sloping nose with a resemblance that has been noted over and over again to a ski jump. In the decades since, the profile created by that logging accident in the Ohio woods had become internationally recognized. And it has become symbolic of a great many things.

It means the cowardly braggart of dozens of films, the craven chump who miraculously finds his courage in time for the final reel . . . the quintessential stand-up comic—richer, more widely traveled, more widely recognized than any of his peers . . . the joke machine, the man who has a marvelously timed one-liner at the ready for every conceivable situation . . . the comic who is all entertainer and little else—the "private" man, if there ever was such a creature, appears to have been swallowed up by the public man long ago . . . the golfaholic . . . the multimillionaire . . . the man who has logged more miles than anyone else to entertain "our guys" in war and peace. In short, it means Bob Hope.

But in 1921 the new face was just another wrinkle in the life of young Leslie Townes Hope, a transplanted Briton from the London suburb of Eltham. It's been said that Hope was not born into poverty (May 29, 1903), but that poverty was soon thrust upon him. His father, William Henry Hope, had always enjoyed a good living as a stonemason. Gradually, however, that began to change. The elder Hope saw demand for his services drop and his income began to suffer.

William Hope relocated his family twice as he searched for work. The first time was in 1905, when the Hopes settled in Bristol. But work failed

to pick up. That's when the senior Hope decided to make the big move—across the Atlantic to the United States. He came over alone in 1906 and, for over a year, he worked and saved his money. By 1908 he was able to send for his wife and six sons. The family arrived in New York City and were soon reunited with the father in Cleveland.

Still, things did not get better for William Hope. He has been characterized on several occasions as a frustrated man caught smack in the middle of the changing times—an Old World fellow unable to come to grips with the changes taking place in the world around him. Eventually, he reportedly gave up trying to make a way for himself as one failure led to another—so he tried to find comfort in alcohol.

Thus it fell to Hope's mother, Avis, to take care of the boys (in the end, there were seven of them) and make the family income. To do this, she took to taking in boarders. Each of the boys understood that it was his responsibility, also, to contribute whatever he could to the family coffers. So as a child, Bob worked at a variety of jobs. He worked in his brother's meat market, sold shoes, hustled pool, caddied, worked as a stock boy and even did some minor league shoplifting. Clues to the course his life would take came early.

One day, for instance, when Bob was selling newspapers on a street corner, one of his regular customers came by in his chauffered limousine and handed the boy a dime for the 2-cent paper. Bob didn't have the necessary change and offered to let the customer settle up the next day. "He wouldn't hear of it," Hope has said, "so I had to run about fifty yards through the rain to a grocery store to break the dime. When I gave him his change, he thanked me and said, 'Always deal in cash, son,' and drove off." The man who dispensed this sage advice was John D. Rockefeller.

Another time, when he was seven, Bob was reciting a poem at a function in Cleveland when he started to flub his lines. The audience laughed and instead of breaking into tears as another child might have done in such a situation, Hope chose instead to exploit what was happening. He began to stumble over line after line to the rising laughter of the audience. Perhaps it was then and there that he found his life's calling.

Initially, though, Hope was a singer, performing in the streets and parks—sometimes with his brothers and sometimes alone—for whatever was collected in a pass of the hat. Occasionally—ever the clown—he would allow his voice to break or wander off-key for the amusement of the audience. Once he signed on as mascot for a local semiprofessional ball team. On road trips he would sing while the team passed the hat on his behalf. In this way, the young mascot often made more than the players.

Hope's early life was one long hustle for cash. Besides making money at odd jobs and by singing, he also took in some income because of his athletic prowess. As a fairly good sprinter, he could usually be counted on to pick up top prize at athletic competitions around Cleveland. Those races that couldn't be won on merit were sometimes run by cheating. For instance, if Hope was to run against a particularly fast adversary, one of his brothers would also enter the race, "accidentally" trip up the adversary and allow Hope to go on to the victory.

It was in high school that Leslie Hope changed his name for the first time. A schoolmate asked the very English-looking student his name and Hope made the mistake of responding, "Hope, Leslie." That, of course, led to endless confrontations and ribbings as the school kids began to refer to him as "Hopelessly" and, later, as plain old "Hopeless." Thus, for a time, Leslie Hope started calling himself Lester Hope instead.

Part of the money Hope scrounged went to saxophone and dance lessons and, before too long, he was so accomplished at the latter that he himself was giving lessons. His prowess was also noted on the amateur vaudeville circuit, where he won a number of talent show top prizes. By the time he left high school, he was a rather accomplished entertainer. Still, that wasn't paying the bills, so he continued working at odd jobs, including a turn on an auto assembly line and as a used car salesman.

There was also a strange turn in Hope's career during which he tried to make a go of it as an amateur boxer. He called himself Packy East, a takeoff on a friend who boxed as Packy West. Hope made it to the semifinals in a local competition, got a forceful introduction to the canvas and

quickly decided to hang up his gloves.

Hope entered vaudeville when he was in his late teens, appearing early on in local houses with a friend, Mildred Rosequist. After Rosequist's family forced her to pull out of the act, Hope found a new partner in another friend, Lloyd Durbin. The boys honed their act in small Cleveland vaudeville houses and then struck out for bigger things. They found those bigger things in a spot on a bill that featured Fatty Arbuckle who, at the time, was in the midst of his comeback campaign.

Hope and Durbin were a hit in that engagement and were signed to a small-time tour of small-town houses in the South. The two young men danced and joked their way through over a year of bus riding, fleabag hotels and unsophisticated audiences for a salary of less than $50 a week each.

However, the team was to end tragically. Durbin ate a coconut cream pie dessert at one stop and died several days later of food poisoning. Hope's next partner was a boy named George Byrne and, together, they billed themselves as "Dancemedians" on the vaudeville circuit. Meanwhile, Hope had begun billing himself differently as well. He decided that "Lester" was bit too highbrow and persnickety for the people he was trying to reach. He needed a chummier, more familiar name. Thus, Leslie became "Bob" Hope. In name, at least.

Becoming Bob Hope in more than name was still some time off. Hope had not yet perfected the snide delivery and split-second timing that were to make him a star. Instead, with George Byrne, he was just another comic performing in baggy pants, oversized shoes and blackface.

Still, that was good enough to take the team of Byrne and Hope to Detroit's State Theatre at $225 a week. Things were to improve even more after that. The pair were booked into the Stanley Theatre in Pittsburgh where their paychecks jumped to $300 a week. It was now or never, the two decided. If they wanted the big time (and they did), then they had to move now, while they still had the momentum. They had to take on New York.

New York flattened the increasingly cocky pair without even breathing hard. Their routine of corny jokes and dance routines simply didn't work in the Big Apple. The up-and-coming young team found itself down and falling in a hurry. Sometimes, the pair weren't even able to get booked at second-rate clubs, let alone top of the line places.

The year was 1927 and twenty-four-year-old Hope was starting to live up to his hated childhood nickname, "Hopeless." Hope and Byrne came close to giving up. Nowadays, of course, Hope can joke about the period, saying that he went $400 in debt for doughnuts and coffee. But it was no joking matter back then.

Salvation of sorts finally came when Hope and his partner landed parts in *The Sidewalks Of New York,* a Broadway musical. The show got good reviews; Hope and Byrne didn't. After the first night, their big spot—a "specialty number" with Ruby Keeler—was yanked from the show. Just a few weeks later, Hope and Byrne suffered a similar fate. The team landed another booking, this time at B. S. Moss Franklin, a top-line theatre. But again, the job didn't last too long and this time the pair decided enough was enough. They got out of New York.

The team's first job outside of the Big Apple was to prove a turning point—for Hope, at least. It was in Newcastle, Pennsylvania, that Hope and Byrne performed their last shows together. The duo were the last performers on a bill with two other acts and, after their performance was over, the manager of the theatre asked Hope to announce coming attractions.

The headliner for the following week was to be a Scotsman, Marshall Walker and his Whiz Bang Revue. Hope made the announcement in a thick Scottish brogue, wisecracking that Walker was such a tightwad he had gotten married in his backyard so his chickens could have the rice. The gag went over well with the audience, and the theatre manager encouraged Hope to expand the routine night after night. Finally, the manager said what had already become painfully obvious. Hope's real talent was as a monologist.

Perhaps Byrne had already seen that as well. He and Hope had a talk and the inevitable split was finalized. The newly solo Hope headed back to Cleveland, put on blackface once more and embarked on a series of one-nighters in and around his hometown. One day, though, he arrived at work too late to apply the blackface only to find, to his surprise, that his audience loved him even more without it. The theatre managers advised him to abandon the blackface because, as they told him, "your face is funny enough without it."

After Cleveland, Hope went to Chicago, where he was booked at the West Englewood Theatre and then at the Stratford. In the process, his salary ballooned from $25 per appearance to $300 a week. After performing at the Stratford for a short while he replaced that theatre's popular MC and held the spot for six months.

Such a long run at the same theatre created a demand for material that Hope had never experienced before. He was forced to develop new material overnight to assure himself of always having something fresh for the Stratford crowd. Hope was not above filling his repertoire with gags borrowed from *College Humor* magazine.

The run at the Stratford also taught Hope an important lesson about timing. As he has since put it, he learned there to make an audience wait for a punch line, thus allowing himself to milk a gag for maximum effectiveness. When Hope left the Stratford, he hired a girl named Louise Troxell to tour with him and feed him straight lines.

Hope and Troxell ended up in Fort Worth, where Bob O'Donnell, the head of the local vaudeville circuit, caught the show. O'Donnell was impressed enough to alert the B. F. Keith office in New York City to send someone to see Hope when he came to the big town. Acting on that high-powered recommendation, Lee Stewart from the Keith office met with Hope and decided to place him in Proctor's 86th Street Theatre. The B. F. Keith office ran the most prestigious circuit in vaudeville and, if Hope did well in this engagement, he knew the sky was his limit. But, for once, doing well was not something that could be taken for granted.

In all truth, there were several factors working against Hope's shot at the big time. Not the least of those factors was his own lack of confidence. Now, with everything lying on the line and his future staring him in the face, Hope was understandably nervous. That nervousness fed on itself and, when Hope undertook a shakedown performance at a small club in Brooklyn, the audience

13

response was dismal. To add to the already bleak picture, Hope was saddled with the knowledge that the crowd at Proctor's was a tough one—even under the best of circumstances.

But somewhere in his mind the daring comic must have counseled himself that, nerves or no, this was It. The Shot. The Chance. If he lost this, he couldn't let it be because he didn't give it his absolute best. On the night Hope finally went onstage at Proctor's, he was preceded by actress Leatrice Joy, who was then in the headlines because of her turbulent marriage to screen star John Gilbert. Thus, when Hope mounted the stage after Joy, he tossed off a daringly flip wisecrack. Pretending to single out a woman in the audience, he informed her: "No, lady. This is not John Gilbert!" The audience loved it.

His future with the Keith Agency was assured, to the happy tune of $450 a week. The agency, true to its reputation, took the young comic straight to the top: Hope managed to fulfill his dream of playing New York's esteemed Palace Theatre. The only problem, however, was that by the late '20s the top was no longer what it had once been in vaudeville. Hope had reached the top just as the art form itself was dying out.

Hope had begun, nevertheless, to attract attention and, for a time, it looked as though the movies would be his next home. A screen test went poorly though, and Hope was forced to look elsewhere for a showcase for his talents. His success in the later days of vaudeville had enabled him to hire writers for the first time and one of them, Al Boasberg, had written a piece called *The Antics of 1931,* in which Hope had a part. He was seen in that show by Al Jolson's manager, Billy Grady, who mentioned Hope to the producers who were casting a show called *The Ballyhoo of 1932.* Those producers liked the comic and gave him a part in the revue.

One night, during an appearance in Newark, the show's opening was delayed and producer Lee Shubert was desperate for something—anything—to keep the crowd from getting restless. Once again, enter Hope and his magic monologue. The comedian, evidencing an encyclopedic memory for jokes that would become his trademark in later years,

entertained the crowd for six long minutes, working with no script or cue cards. The applause was so fervent that Hope's monologue was written in as a regular part of the show. *Ballyhoo,* though, closed without much ballyhoo just a few months later.

Still, *Ballyhoo* proved to be a stepping stone to a bigger and better relationship between Bob Hope and Broadway. The next year Hope was cast in *Roberta.* One of his best-remembered quips is from that show: "Long dresses don't bother me. I've got a good memory." The show drew rave reviews.

Broadway wasn't the only aspect of Hope's career that was booming during the '30s. Although he must have felt a sense of being a big fish in an ever-shrinking pond, the fact is that he was still doing quite well in vaudeville, filling the time between Broadway runs with road trips.

Despite his earlier disastrous screen test, Hope and films continued to feel one another out. It was in 1934, while Hope was appearing in *Roberta,* that he was approached by Educational Pictures to play in a short film. The company also dangled an option for five other films if the first, titled *Going Spanish,* was successful. Hope himself wasn't happy with his work in the finished film, though, and before any outside forces could sink the picture, he himself took deadly aim. He ran into influential columnist Walter Winchell at a showing of the film and when Winchell asked him for an appraisal of *Going Spanish,* Hope quipped: "When they catch John Dillinger, public enemy number one, they're going to make him sit through it twice." An angry and surprised Educational Pictures promptly dropped him!

Right after that, however, Warner Brothers decided to give Hope a try, signing him for a series of shorts. Between 1934 and 1938 the comedian made *The Old Gray Mayor; Paree, Paree; Watch The Birdie; Double Exposure; Calling All Tars; Shop Talk* and *Don't Hook Now.* That last film is of special significance to cinematic trivia buffs. In it, Hope played himself and was teamed for the first time on film with singer Bing Crosby.

It wasn't the first time, though, that the two had worked together. That milestone had come earlier, in a 1932 vaudeville show at the Capitol Theatre. That performance was noteworthy for another rea-

14

Bob and the beautiful Dolores were married in Erie, Pennsylvania in early 1934.

son, too; it was the one that launched what would turn out to be a long love affair between Hope and the new medium of radio.

In the early '30s radio was largely seen as the giant killer that was slaying vaudeville. Such accusations, of course, set a pattern that repeats and lingers to this day. In later years television was accused of killing off radio and films and then pay-TV was charged with flattening both television and films. But at the time, as the Depression deepened and millions of Americans found that they could afford no entertainment more extravagant than an evening

Bob and Dolores in Vaudeville.

spent huddling around the big box in the living room, radio was king. And any performer who wanted to go on performing had to accept that fact.

The Hope performance at the Capitol was a lucky one for him, because the Capitol was owned by the Loew's Corporation, which booked him to appear on the Capitol Family Hour, a Sunday morning show. That led to guest appearances and feature spots on *The Fleischman Hour, RKO Theater Of*

The Air and the *Bromo Seltzer Intimate Hour.*

Hope's career wasn't the only part of his life that was going great guns during the '30s. He had the money and the looks to live it up in style and he became a self-confessed playboy. He has joked that the girls piled onto the running boards of his Pierce-Arrow town car. "I was single, I had a car with these beautiful low fenders and I had all the girls in New York. All the showgirls!"

That lasted until the night Hope and George Murphy, a co-star from *Roberta,* happened into the Vogue Club in New York as songstress Dolores Reade was performing. The cocky playboy and man-about-town found himself in love, chasing the beautiful young singer until she caught him. "She got me hooked," he has said, "and then went to Florida to work. So I had a telephone growing out of my ear, trying to keep in touch with her. Dolores made me like it that way."

The two were married in early 1934 in Erie, Pennsylvania. They performed together occasionally in vaudeville revues until Dolores retired and embarked upon a new career—being Mrs. Bob Hope.

The '30s, the decade when everything finally came together for Bob Hope, was also the decade of tragic loss. In 1934 Hope's mother died of cancer. She had been, arguably, the single most important influence on his early development, the one who believed in him when others didn't. Even his brothers hadn't shared her faith. In fact, Hope says his brothers were united in their conviction that he'd never amount to anything in show business—a conviction that apparently endured until the day one of those brothers saw Hope receive a check for $20,000. "My brother looked over my shoulder and his eyes popped. He looked at me, *smiled* at me, for the first time since I was born. Shortly afterward, he was borrowing money from me and started his company—the Hope Metal company! Can you imagine?!"

Avis Townes Hope, on the other hand, was a believer. She didn't live to see the $20,000 check, but that didn't matter. Hope often recalls the time she took him to see comedian Frank Fay and, in the middle of Fay's act, announced to her son in a loud voice, "He's not *half* as good as you!" Just a few years after she died, Hope's father died, too.

17

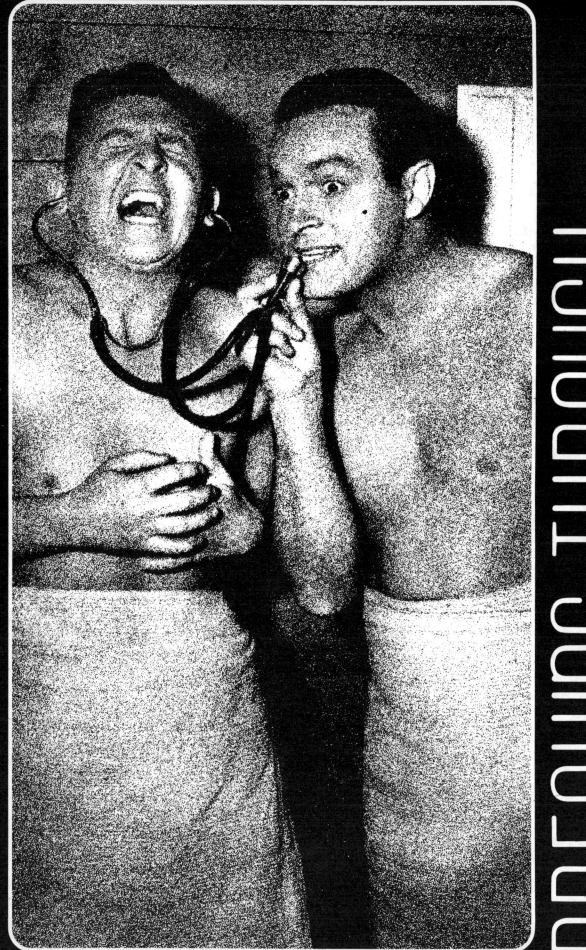

BREAKING THROUGH

CHAPTER 2 ●

RADIO AND FILMS both finally opened up for Bob Hope at about the same time—the late '30s. In fact, it was in 1937 that he was signed to do the *Woodbury Soap Show*; later that year, he also got his first big movie assignment—*The Big Broadcast of 1938*. The fact that the film and the radio show were underway simultaneously created a logistics problem in that they were produced on opposite coasts. That problem was solved by having Hope host his radio show from Hollywood via the first transcontinental hookup.

Still, the broadcast presented other problems that had to be overcome. As a performer with roots in vaudeville, Hope had had trouble getting used to the notion of playing to a microphone instead of an audience. He and other transplanted vaudevillians needed—and got—live studio audiences for their radio broadcasts. That created difficulty once Hope was in Hollywood, simply because no one had been informed of his need for a live audience. Hope didn't find this out until it was too late, and he was panic-stricken. True to his fears, the first show had an audience of about four, and he bombed miserably.

There was nothing to do except to hijack an audience. And that's precisely what the wily comic did. By the time the second radio hookup rolled around, Hope had arranged things with an usher. The *Char-lie McCarthy Show* was taping down the hall from Hope's studio, and McCarthy's broadcast ended fifteen minutes before Hope's was scheduled to begin. With the aid of the usher, Hope arranged ropes leading out of McCarthy's studio and straight into his own. Hope met the confused and shanghaied crowd at the door, found them seats and started his broadcast. He was a hit.

After the twenty-six-week run of the *Woodbury Soap Show*, Hope joined a show called *Your Hollywood Parade*. The show didn't last long, but Hope got favorable reviews. Pepsodent, the toothpaste maker, noticed and signed him as host of its new radio program, *The Pepsodent Show*.

That proved to be Hope's introduction to big time radio. In an era dominated by veteran radio funnymen like Jack Benny and Edgar Bergen, Hope came on fast and strong. Radio audiences caught on to his rapid-fire style of sardonic monologue, and they liked what they heard.

Hope's writers created and discarded a veritable mountain of material for each radio broadcast, all in search of the "perfect" thirty minutes of laughs. The comedian's humor was also very much a thing of the moment, as he developed and refined his trademark penchant for weaving his routines around current headlines. The irreverent topicality of his material often gave Pepsodent reason to shiver. For instance, there was the time show regular Jerry Colonna, as Santa Claus, was killed off by Hope. The episode lit up the network's switchboards; letters and telegrams soon followed, all from angered listeners. But Hope managed to survive that episode, as well as others involving "blue" comedy that fell right on the fringes of what was then considered bad taste.

In retrospect, Hope's radio shows were a daffy, schtick-laden potpourri of gags pulled off by a team that included, besides the comedian himself, Vera Vague (played by Barbara Jo Allen), Blanche Stewart, Elvira Allman, Brenda Frazier, Cobina Wright, Jr., and thick-moustached, pop-eyed Colonna. Hope also showcased the talents of the vocal group Six Hits and a Miss, as well as singers Judy Garland and Doris Day.

Many of the show's most memorable moments were instigated by Colonna. His masterpiece during his years with Hope is widely conceded to be Yehudi, the mythical man Colonna would play on each week's episode. Yehudi was the guy who performed such mysterious and indispensable services as shutting off the light in the refrigerator once the door was closed. To the apparent surprise of both Hope and Colonna, Yehudi became a major success and quite a few gags wound up being built around him.

Bob Hope on the radio was quite a bit like Hope on film: a conceited fop with nothing whatsoever to be conceited about, and a wisecracking smart aleck with an appropriate gag ever at the ready. And, again, just like in his films, Hope found widespread audience favor because of his ability to milk those alleged character flaws for laughs.

Radio is also the place where the famous Crosby-Hope feud was first refined and used as a laugh-getting tool. The two quip masters went at one another tooth and nail and, just like on film, their timing was a thing of wonder. Hope zinged Crosby about the size of his ears, the quality (or lack of same) of his singing, his age and his need to wear a toupee. Crosby would come right back with pointed observations on Hope's nose, his routines, and his success (or lack of same) with the ladies.

The long-running Hope and Crosby rivalry on-stage masked a deep and abiding affection. When word reached him in 1977 that Crosby had died on a golf course in Spain, Hope says his head got

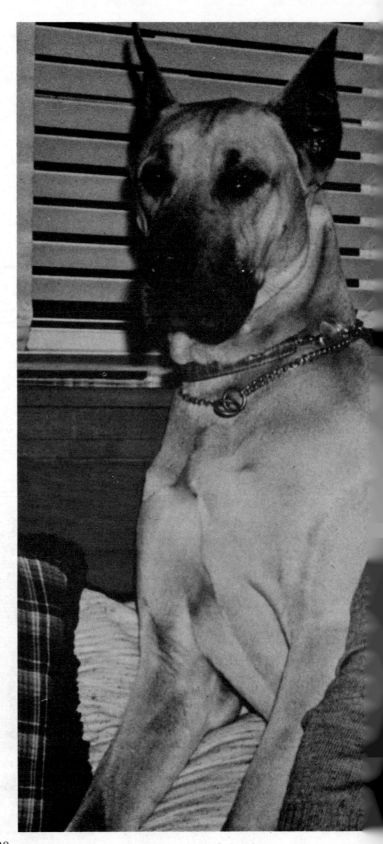

20

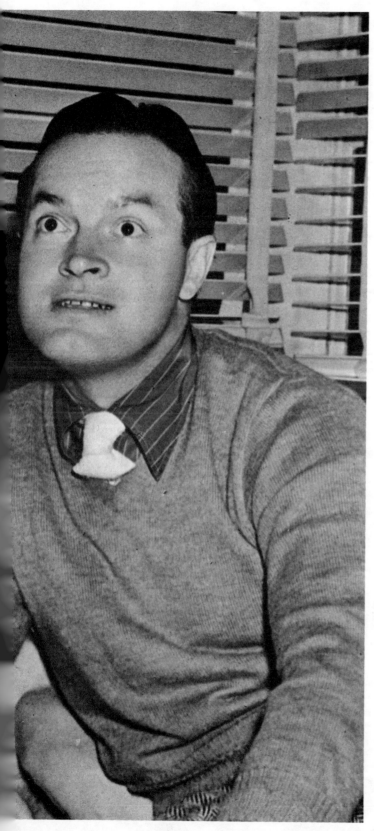

"tight"—so much so that it felt dangerous. "I didn't cry at all. I don't cry easily. I just felt that tightness, and I felt the whole shock of it deeply."

Many of Hope's radio shows originated from whatever military base he happened to be visiting at the time. Typically, he also managed to weave plenty of references to life on that military base into his monologue.

After the war, as the '40s steamed toward a close, Hope's radio popularity started to wane. In a 1948 attempt to stem that tide, the comic dropped his old sidekicks and opened the new season with an entirely new company. He also found himself with a new sponsor, as Pepsodent dropped out to be replaced by Lever Brothers, the soap makers.

Five years later, Hope revamped again. This time he signed on with General Foods to provide five 15-minute morning shows during the weekdays and one half-hour weekend show. That move staved off the inevitable for another five years but, in the end, even the once-invincible Hope could not resist the tide.

It was painfully simple. Twenty years before, radio had helped to end vaudeville's glory days. Now television—the Boob Tube, the Idiot Box, the Electronic Babysitter—was on the rise and radio performers like Hope could choose to either join the march or be crushed underneath it.

But Hope and television didn't hit it off right away. Early on there was a lot of hesitancy—a lot of feeling one another out. Much of that tentativeness was on Hope's part, as he attempted to figure out how to best deal with the prominent new medium.

Bob's first television experience happened in the early '30s, decades before he went to work doing regular "specials" for NBC. At that time he was working for CBS, guesting on one of the network's earliest broadcasts.

Nineteen forty-seven found Hope back on television and making history. He was part of the first commercial television broadcast on the West Coast, opening the show with characteristically topical gags. Just a few years later he was ready to take the plunge, signing on with NBC. His schedule made it impossible for him to undertake a regular series like many of his contemporaries were doing, so he and the network hit on the idea of the Bob Hope specials, of which he would do about nine a year.

The first Bob Hope special went on the air on Easter Sunday, 1950. The lavishly budgeted production featured among its guest stars Douglas Fairbanks, Jr. and Dinah Shore. But even such a cast was not enough to stop critics and self-appointed media watchdogs from pouncing. One commonly held viewpoint among the latter group was that the show simply wasn't suitable fare for proper Christians.

Nonetheless, Hope, who had a five-show pact with his sponsor, Frigidaire, was back with his second special just a few weeks later, with guests Peggy Lee and Frank Sinatra. The critics were kinder this time, but it was apparent that Hope had a long way to go before he was comfortable enough with this new medium to be able to mold and use it as he had vaudeville, radio, Broadway, and films.

In the theatre, where he might appear as an ant-sized speck to the patron sitting in the back row of the balcony, the performer is taught to play up otherwise minute gestures and move so that everyone in the audience will get the full impact of what's going on. And that's fine, for theatre. But that very training is what makes it so difficult for theatrical performers to transplant their acts to television. What looks perfectly natural and normal in theatre is dreadfully hammy overacting on television.

The problem lies in the nature of the medium. Television is a more intimate art form; what works elsewhere will not work on the tube. Hope has conceded that television once frightened him—not only because it didn't mesh with his style of comedy, but also because he didn't mesh well with *it,* wasn't used to the armies of technicians, cameramen and script people that are crucial to every television shot.

Eventually, of course, he got the hang of it all, becoming proficient enough to last out over thirty years of specials with NBC. The most remarkable thing about those Hope specials is the fact that they haven't changed much over the years. Like their star, they benefit from a certain comfortable familiarity that, contrary to the old saying, has yet to breed

contempt. On the contrary, Hope's shows usually score at or near the top of the Nielsen ratings.

Hope has constructed his TV specials formula out of the simplest of elements, out of things that wouldn't work in anyone else's hands. One of the first things he did was to slow down and re-pace his monologues, learning as he went how to make the visual aspect of the medium work for him and not against him.

Then he hit upon the idea of building each one of the shows around a particular theme—vaudeville, Broadway, his leading ladies, his birthdays, NASA, Christmas in Vietnam, and so on. Without this device, it's doubtful the shows would have survived as long as they have, simply because the audience, at one point or another, would have grown tired of the whole thing. But by making the programs into "salutes" Hope manages to keep each special special.

Finally, of course, the comedian has always believed in the use of high-powered talent to co-star with him. Thus he has shared the stage with the likes of Lucille Ball, Jack Benny, Brooke Shields, George Burns, Bing Crosby, Phyllis Diller, Cheryl Tiegs, Milton Berle, Jimmy Durante, Danny Thomas, Eva Gabor, Sammy Davis, Jr., John Davidson, Raquel Welch, Petula Clark and Tom Jones, among many others.

Additionally, and in keeping with his desire to feature names that are in the news, Hope also includes on his specials such people as 1972 Olympic gold medalist Mark Spitz and, in 1983, astronauts Sally Ride (the nation's first woman in space) and Guy Buford (the first black in space). Therefore, like the radio shows of old, Hope's television specials lean heavily on current events gags—as well as on the usual generous serving of corny wit.

It's a testament to Hope's awesome staying power that he and those gags are still embraced by Americans after so many years and so many media. If anything, it would seem that television, that medium that brings performers into our homes week after week, month after month, until they become almost part of the family, would have robbed Hope of some of his appeal after so many years. But the

tube hasn't burned him out. His durability remains intact.

Start trying to unravel the secret of that durability and you find yourself tackling riddles that have no set solution. Sixty years onstage—thirty of them on television . . . it simply can't be done. It's flat-out impossible. Except . . .

Except that nobody told Bob Hope that and, from his early, faltering beginnings, he has mastered television like no one else. If anything, the medium has added to—not detracted from—his staying power. He has remained welcome in American homes for reasons so deceptively simple they can easily be overlooked. The big name guests help keep him current. And his own ability keeps him sufficiently down to earth so people don't grow tired of his repeat visits to their living room.

In that sense, Hope is like a favorite old uncle who's always welcome for dinner, bringing presents for the little ones and table wine for mom and dad. He is, simultaneously, the bigger-than-life hero with a face that probably belongs on Mt. Rushmore, and the guy next door, facing life's little catastrophies with a bouyant attitude and sharp wit everyone else wishes they had.

Simply put, Hope is a personable hero, a man who communicates with but never talks down to his audience. As a TV comic, he's a proven commodity. People know they will like him, because they have liked him so many times before.

As mentioned before, Hope often plumbs his own life for themes to the TV specials. For example, in 1958 and again in 1969, he brought his TV audiences revivals of his early '30s Broadway smash, *Roberta* (with Janis Paige, Howard Keel and Anna Maria Alberghetti in 1958; Paige, John Davidson and Michele Lee in 1969).

Hope has also centered specials around his film career and around his leading ladies. The latter aired in 1966 with Lucille Ball, Joan Fontaine, Joan Collins, Virginia Mayo, Hedy Lamarr, Janis Paige, and Dorothy Lamour, among others.

The always welcomed Christmas specials often emanated from whatever military outpost Hope happened to be visiting at the time. When that tradition ended in 1972, Hope joked that he missed the excitement of getting ready to leave. Like, for instance,

when the Army gave the troupe the necessary shots: "On a good day," said he, "they used me as a lawn sprinkler."

Occasionally Hope's specials have made history of a sort. For instance, in 1958 his theme was Russian entertainment in a show that was filmed in Moscow by the Soviets. It took endless hours of negotiation to overcome the many objections the Russians broached to the project. Even after the project was approved, Hope's monologue turned out to be a source of Kremlin controversy because his jokes mocked certain unmockable aspects of Soviet life.

Nearly two decades later, Hope was at it again. This time, he was in China, which had just resumed relations with the United States. Hope spent a curious month in the People's Republic, where he was basically regarded as just another American. The years China had spent closed off to Western influence meant that the Chinese man-on-the-street didn't know or care anything about Bob Hope.

There had been some initial worries that Hope's showman's ego might get a tad riled at being passed over in the street without so much as a request for an autograph or two. He insisted, however, that the situation was quite the opposite. "It's a rest," he said, "a great cure for the big head."

Just as the Russian officials had done in 1958, the Chinese in 1976 didn't make things easy for Hope. Officials from the Culture Ministry scrutinized his material daily, demanding the removal of any scenes that they considered condescending or risqué.

The officials also raised objections to the fact that Hope's Chinese co-stars were being allowed to play only subservient roles. "It didn't seem to make any difference," said Hope, "that the joke was always at my expense. We changed some things around, because I certainly did not intend to insult anyone."

Hope called the China trip the only true "road" project he'd ever done, since the movies with Crosby had all been filmed on a Paramount backlot. And if that's true, then this particular road was bumpier

than any the wisecracking duo ever encountered at Paramount. Hope was under constant electronic surveillance while he was in China, which moved him to quip to reporters upon his return, "Every time I left the room, I said to the floor lamp, 'Goodbye—we're leaving now.' "

Resuscitating a joke he had used in connection with the Soviet project. Hope also noted that he didn't have any trouble with the language while he was in China "because nobody talked to me."

The comedian's visit to China marked some especially poignant moments for the Chinese performers allowed to participate in the making of the show. For years, under the Cultural Revolution, Chinese entertainers were forbidden to perform. One Chinese comedy team that worked with Hope on the special had had it especially rough. One of the duo had worked for ten years as a doorman; his partner had been imprisoned.

Hope told a newspaper reporter, "They haven't had much chance to practice their craft, but their timing is as good as you'd expect from professionals anywhere. Timing tells. They could have been Laurel and Hardy."

The American television crew had their pick of historical sites to shoot at. Hope brought along a uniquely American entourage, including country singer Crystal Gayle, the singers Peaches and Herb, the mime team of Shields and Yarnell, and even Carroll Spinney, a.k.a. Big Bird from *Sesame Street*.

Upon his return Hope told reporters that he'd found the Chinese to be "cooperative." "That country," he said, "is going to be something to contend with. It's really moving."

Nineteen eighty-three brought with it a truly special Hope special—an eightieth birthday salute. The three-hour show took place at the Kennedy Center in Washington and, for once, it didn't feature Hope at center stage anchoring goofy skits or chasing voluptuous women. In fact, for most of the evening, Hope wasn't onstage at all. He was in the President's box with Ronald and Nancy Reagan as guest after guest mounted the stage below to offer a tribute, roast the host a little, or share an anecdote about the man being honored.

Turning eighty found Hope in his traditional good health and spirits. The thing that was most impressive, though, is the fact that, even at that advanced age, Hope still refused to talk of slowing down. In fact, he still has goals he'd like to get to "someday" —for instance, a film biography of Walter Winchell, a Hope directorial debut.

There's something refreshing in all of that—something life-affirming. Like George Burns, seven years his senior, Hope has pretty much refused to acknowledge the passing of the years. He quips about it, to be sure. And sometimes, when he expresses views that predate World War II, the realization strikes like a freight train—forget the illusions he has created: this is an old man.

But what separates Bob Hope from other old men is his refusal to immerse himself in his age, to become some wrinkled old codger still living on yesterday's glories and triumphs. On the whole, Hope has managed to remain a man very much rooted in today—the present. And nowhere was that as apparent as on the birthday special when, in the midst of such sexy young beauties as Cheryl Tiegs, Brooke Shields, Ann Jillian and Christie Brinkley, he managed the neat trick of not coming off as either father figure or dirty old man. Just a guy who's still crazy for the ladies after all these years.

"Security is really tight in the President's box," said Hope, coming onstage to a thunderous ovation. "One agent checked me for bombs and threw out half my monologue." The line—a clinker in anyone else's hands, a howler coming from Hope— was quiet proof that the master comic still had his stuff—even at eighty.

Although the bulk of Hope's television appearances have been on his own specials, he has not limited himself to them. He has served a number of times as host for the annual Academy Awards show (he says it's known at his house as "Passover," a reference to the fact that, although he has won a handful of special Oscars, he has never won one of the statuettes on the strength of his own film performance).

In addition to the Academy Awards show, Hope is a frequent guest on the talk show circuit. He often arranges trade-offs with guests who appear on his specials, promising that if they appear free of charge on his show, he will return the favor.

26

(below) Steppin out with the girls. (right) "My Favorite Blonde" with Madeleine Carroll.

Hope has also remained quite active in the area of commercial advertising, acting as spokesman for California Federal Savings and Texaco gas and oil products. Although the idea of a star of Hope's stature doing commercials might once have been considered a tremendous comedown, Hope is not alone as a pitchman. Such established stars as George Burns, Dennis Weaver, Michael Landon, Alan Alda and Bill Cosby have also been identifying themselves with products more closely than once they might have. And, as Hope himself cracks, the money is good.

"Making commercials is big business today," he says. "When you see Laurence Olivier selling Pola-roids and Gregory Peck pushing Travelers Insurance, you know it's something everybody's getting into."

The format for the spots is similar to what has worked for Hope for most of his life. There is either a skit of the type you might see on a Hope special, or else the pitch is dressed up like a segment of a Hope monologue. For Cal-Fed, for instance, one spot started out: "Someone once called me the funniest man in the world. I think it was me. But I get very serious when it comes to saving money . . ."

After signing to do the Cal-Fed spot, Hope quipped, "Today the stars are making the commercials and the unknowns are making the movies."

27

THE WAR YEARS

CHAPTER 3 ●

As THE LEGEND goes, Bob Hope tried to enlist in the armed forces when World War II finally stretched to the United States. But, supposedly, the comic was told that he could better serve the country by helping to maintain the morale of the fighting men.

Hope apparently took that advice to heart, because in the years since it was given he has logged more miles than any other performer in the campaign to bring entertainment to "our boys." The tours took Hope to tiny, forgotten military outposts and even into the thick of the action, within earshot of the enemy.

In the process, Hope became indelibly identified with the USO tours, and they became as much an American institution as he is himself. During the '40s that identification made Hope a hero, the rich and popular celebrity who was neither too rich, too popular, nor too much the celebrity to risk his life making others happy.

It started for Hope on May 6, 1941. The war clouds that had broken over Europe were now gathered ominously over the United States. The world was watching anxiously to see how long the democratic superpower could avoid being drawn into the conflict. That question would, of course, be answered almost seven months to the day later in the Japanese air raid at Pearl Harbor, Hawaii. But on

that day in May the nation was still technically at peace as Bob Hope entertained his first set of troops.

World War II has been called the last "clean" war, and although no armed conflict between nations can ever be truly clean, this war deserved that title more than most. It was a war of neatly drawn lines, of peace- and freedom-loving Americans finally forced into action against an enemy so terrifyingly epic in its evil that no rational person could see any alternative. Perhaps that's why American men responded with such fervent eagerness to the call to arms, and why American women were content to work in war plants and ration food for the duration.

That's also why Hope was so widely hailed as a hero for what he did. What he did took him away from his family and, on more than one occasion, nearly cost him his life. "The first Christmas show was in Alaska," recalls Hope, "in '42 and we almost got killed getting there. Our plane was flying from Cordova to Anchorage. We were never going to fly at night, but they were having a street dance in Anchorage in our honor, so we had to.

"But we ran into a storm over Anchorage and the radio went out. We had our Mae Wests on. We couldn't see anything. Then a United Airlines plane felt our backwash and radioed the base and they turned on the antiaircraft lights and the pilot saw the beam. It was a relief to land."

Another time, Hope and scriptwriter Hal Block were writing gags in their hotel room during a bomb run. Block said, "We did a show and ran for our lives." Hope's retort: "I've never done anything else."

Once, 600 men marched ten miles across the moors to reach Hope's next stop after he passed up their camp. The guys were out of luck once again, though, reaching the next camp after the performance there was over. When Hope heard about the soldiers he rounded up his troupe, caught the hikers and gave a forty-minute show—in the rain.

His wartime adventures have left Hope with a storehouse of anecdotes like that one—some of them funny, others touching, and a few downright sad. Like, for instance, the time Hope and crew were en route to a show in Sydney, and developed engine trouble crossing a mountain range. The plane started losing power at an alarming rate and the pilot was casting about desperately for a place to land. The entertainers in the back started jettisoning everything they could find—even luggage—to lighten the load and try to keep the plane in the air.

Suddenly the pilot yelled back to the troupe . . . he had found a small bay—but the landing was going to be rough. Singer Frances Langford strapped herself into her seat, while Hope and other members of the crew braced themselves as best they could on the floor. The plane limped down on one motor, slapping the surface of the water hard before skipping twice, like a stone. It was a bumpy landing but no one was hurt. They found themselves in the eastern Australian town of Laurieton.

In 1945 Hope's troupe performed for American GIs stationed in Kassel, Germany, and staying in a hotel that probably served as a living memorial to the brutality of war. The building had only three sides; the fourth had been destroyed by a bomb.

It was during a visit to Algiers that Hope and company first encountered General Dwight Eisenhower, who assured them that the American hold on the territory was firm. For Hope and the bomb-weary members of his troupe, that came as especially good news. It meant a night's sleep uninterrupted by the crashing thunder of bombs.

Or so they thought. At 4 A.M., the air raid sirens sounded and the bombs fell, forcing the entertainers to flee to a wine cellar for shelter. The next day Hope sent Eisenhower a wire thanking him for the rest. His pen dripping with sarcasm, Hope wrote to the President-to-be, "I'm glad I wasn't here on one of the nights when you had some action."

Webster's defines jungle rot as "any skin disease or affliction, as a fungus, prevalent in tropical climates." Hope would probably have had a few other well-chosen words of description which, if they lacked the technical precision of the dictionary, would have been at least twice as colorful.

It was during a trip to Dutch New Guinea in 1944 that Hope first got the disease—on his feet. It tortured him for years afterward whenever the weather was humid, despite all efforts of the best doctors.

Hope likes to tell the story of the time he and his troupe beat the Marines in landing at Wonsan during the later Korean War. The comedians and dancers found a ghost town when they landed; not a soul in sight to greet them. Finally, some twenty minutes later, the U.S. First Marine Division arrived on the scene. Both parties were mutually shocked by the presence of the other! It turned out that the planeload of entertainers had landed during a bloodless invasion by the Marines and had been surrounded the whole time by guerrillas without ever knowing it.

Besides the appearances for troops in the field, Hope also made it a practice to go to the hospitals and visit with soldiers too sick to attend the shows. He'd saunter in amongst maimed, burned, blinded, crippled and dying boys with a jaunty, "Don't get up," or else he'd order them to break out the dice so he could get a crap game going.

Those hospital visits often touched off moments of affecting poignancy. In one instance, a wounded kid broke out in loud crying while Frances Langford was singing. Hope broke the awkward silence that followed by saying, "Fellas, the folks at home are having a terrible time about eggs. They can't get any powdered eggs at all. They've got to use the old-fashioned kind you break open." It wasn't much of a joke, but under the circumstances, it was a lifesaver.

Another time, there was no ready quip, just a kid

in a hospital in Tokyo who wouldn't talk. Hope, who was taking home numbers from all the soldiers so he could call their families when he got stateside again, couldn't get the kid to give up the information, "so I patted him and said OK. Later the nurse came over and said he wanted to talk to me. He said, 'Would you really call my folks?' " Hope did and, a year later, he chanced to see the kid again, apparently cured of all physical and mental scars.

There was a badly injured boy on the island of Espiritu Santo that Hope probably remembers with bittersweet emotion. He was receiving a transfusion, which prompted Hope to walk up to his bed and quip, "I see they're giving you a little pick-me-up?" The kid was game. He retorted, "It's only raspberry soda, but it feels pretty good." Two hours later a doctor approached Hope to tell him that the boy had just died. Being game apparently hadn't been enough.

The shows that Hope took to those godforsaken theatres of combat were vintage vaudeville, full of the stars of the day and typical Hope zingers. "Were the soldiers at the last camp happy to see me!" Hope told one audience. "They actually got down on their knees. What a spectacle! What a tribute! What a crap game!"

In a 1944 radio broadcast from the Navy Ground School at Point Loma, Hope told the one about the workman at a training station who was replacing the doors on the barracks. "He said, 'I put new doors on this place every six weeks. It's a boot camp, and when the boys graduate, they don't wait to turn the knobs.' "

In 1945, at Camp Cooke, Hope joked about his ride on a troop train. "That's a crap game with a caboose. I won't say the train was old, but between Chicago and Kansas City, Jesse James held it up three times. These tankmen were very disgusted with the engineer. Everytime they went over a deep canyon they'd say, 'He must be getting soft . . . he's using the bridge.' "

In 1970 Hope joked for the first time about the then-hot topic of marijuana with an audience of soldiers in Vietnam. "I hear you fellows are interested in gardening," he quipped. "Our CO tells us you grow a lot of grass. . . . Instead of taking it [grass] away from the soldiers, we should be giving

Entertaining the Air Force in Thailand.

31

it to the negotiators in Paris."

Although they have been less publicized than Hope, the fact is the entertainers who made those countless tours with him were self-sacrificing heroes and heroines in their own right. Take for instance, in 1942, when Hope decided to follow in the footsteps of Joe E. Brown and Edgar Bergen, who had been to entertain the troops in Alaska. When Frances Langford offered to join Hope, her husband voiced an objection, reminding her that she had symptoms of acute appendicitis. Her reply: "They have doctors in Alaska too." That settled the argument.

A few years after the war, Alaska figured in another trip by the Hope team. The comedian was asked by then-Secretary of the Air Force Stuart Symington to make a holiday visit to U.S. troops in Anchorage. Hope attempted to beg off with the excuse that he had been absent from home the Christmas before, bringing yule cheer to the troops. This year, he explained, he wanted to stay home with his wife and kids.

But it turned out that both wife and kids were thrilled with the idea of spending Christmas in a real, live winter wonderland, so Hope had no choice but to relent. There was, however, one other problem. The plane to Alaska was leaving that very day, giving Hope all of about five hours to put together his troupe. It turned out not to be as much of a problem as it sounded. With just a few phone calls, Hope managed to line up singing cowboy Jimmy Wakeley, pianist Jeff Clarkson and dancer Patty Thomas.

The landing in Anchorage was another minor miracle. The plane ran into a thick fog, and the pilot had to be talked down by the tower. Hope recalls that after the tower radioed that they were on line for touchdown and on their own, he still couldn't see anything. And, to top things off, it was nearly 30 degrees below freezing. Luckily, the plane set down in the fog without a hitch. Hope and crew did a dozen shows and, in the process, the comedian caught a nasty cold and lost his voice.

Once, during World War II, a rare thing happened. Hope the ham was upstaged. And the culprit, surprisingly enough, wasn't a singer, dancer or comedian. It was a rodent. A mouse, to be exact.

It happened during a performance at an amphitheatre in Tarawa. Hope was onstage entertaining his audience of Marines when he noticed that he was beginning to lose their attention. All eyes had focused on an electrical wire stretched across the stage; there was a mouse on that wire, trying to make its way across. Hope tried to get the audience's attention back, but it was no use. Finally, and perhaps sensing the odor of defeat, Hope stopped the show, waited until the tiny highwire act was over (the mouse crossed safely) and then continued.

One of the things that endeared Hope to the fighting men he entertained was his apparent ability to blend in and become just one of the boys—a pal the soldiers genuinely liked instead of some brass stuffed-shirt they were ordered to respect. He recalls fondly, for instance, the times he was piped aboard a U.S. vessel in an impressive show of pomp, only to have the formality of the whole affair punctured by sailors who greeted him like a long-lost buddy: "Hi, Niblick Nose! Hi, Ski Snoot!"

Another time, in Bone, Africa, the camaraderie of the soldiers was the primary element in resuscitating the comedian after a series of air raids and run-for-your-life-because-the-enemy-is-coming performances had left him tired, dirty, and more than a little scared. Hope had wrenched his knee by leaping for cover during an air raid, so he had to use a cane to limp onstage. The soldiers could see that he was in trouble as he started his show with the customary, "Good afternoon, everybody."

That brought a gruff retort from way in back: "Hi ya, slacker!" Both the audience and Hope howled, and he zinged right back with, "It's amazing how you meet Crosby's relatives everywhere." One eyewitness says the heckler was better for Hope than a tonic. According to that eyewitness, from that moment Hope underwent a physical change you could actually *see*; he was his old self again, and he was ready to go.

Hope himself has called the incident an example of "soldier's humor," the emblem of men who have shared a rough experience together. Crying and sentimental commiseration are out of place in such circumstances, according to Hope. The soldiers express themselves and *help* themselves with comradely hu-

34

mor—no sympathy allowed.

Stateside, Hope's Korean and World War II adventures—to say nothing of his many peacetime visits to military bases—established him as an authentic American hero. As *Time* put it in 1943, "For fighting men, this grimmest of wars is in one small way also the gayest." It is, of course, ludicrous to think of any war in terms of gayness, but certainly, the observation makes its point. As one homesick soldier said, seeing Hope and crew clowning onstage was like having the United States in front of you again for an hour.

Probably the biggest fuss raised about those old tours was from some fundamentalists who objected to Hope's use of pretty girls in revealing outfits to get a rise from the guys. Hope labeled those critics "partypoopers," saying that the girls were there to inspire the soldiers and let them see what they were fighting for.

Occasionally those boys were lucky enough to get unexpectedly close to "what they were fighting for." In Vietnam, for example, one nervous young soldier got the chance to serenade a beauty queen with his rendition of "You're Just Too Wonderful," while Hope and a bunch of envious GIs looked on and offered encouragement.

One show took the Hope troupe to a ball field on Okinawa. It had rained recently, leaving the field so muddy that volunteers were solicited to carry the women in the show bodily from their jeeps to the stage. Needless to say, there was no shortage of young men ready, willing and able to lend a helping hand, and the whole thing was ultimately decided in a few quick, unscheduled boxing matches.

Hope is fond of telling the eerie story of the time he and Dolores were in Berlin in 1948 as part of the Airlift Show. It was on Christmas day that a man approached Hope and identified himself as a disc jockey broadcasting to the European Theatre. He invited the comedian to drop by the studio for an on-air interview and Hope agreed.

As it turned out, Hope didn't remember the promise until two o'clock the next morning, following a big dinner with some military and diplomatic officials. Nonetheless, on his way back to his hotel, the comedian started to search out the address he had scratched out on a card. Berlin was then a city of

rubble, and gasoline was scarce. Thus, when their staff car ran out of gas, Hope and his wife were forced to get out and walk, picking their way by the meager light of a flashlight over and around chunks of buildings, burned-out cars, and people—both alive and dead—pinned in the debris.

When the two finally walked in on the disc jockey, he was flabbergasted. Before the comedian knew what had happened, the young man had shoved the mike at him and run to arouse the other disc jockeys who, like him, manned the station in rotating one-hour shifts. Hope and the station personnel kicked back, there in the wee hours of the morning in war-torn Berlin, and talked for a while about everything that came to mind.

The souvenirs Hope brought home from his wartime tours are many and varied. He reportedly has tons of enemy guns and flags, along with rooms full of trophies, medals, plaques and statues. President Truman sent Hope a million "Thanks for the Memory" signatures from World War II GIs. In addition to these artifacts, Hope has many others, some unique.

There is, for instance, a sheet of stamps bearing Hitler's likeness, printed during the war but never issued. Hope also managed to secure some of der Fuehrer's personal stationery and, perhaps most priceless of all in many ways, a photo of General George Patton fulfilling a promise to urinate in the Rhine.

Hope, dubbed America's "Number One Soldier in Greasepaint" by *Variety,* curtailed his USO activities in the early 1970s. By then the controversy over American involvement in Vietnam was at its height and many people took to using the comedian as a target for venting their frustrations against that unpopular war. Hope, saddened and surprised, continued his Vietnam tours anyway, entertaining the troops at a time when many other performers were finding it professionally, politically and personally easier to stay at home. Hope kept doing what he believed in, what he had been doing for some thirty-odd years. There's a certain element of heroism in that.

Critics said he was a war lover. Hope responded that no man who had seen as much combat as he, who had smelled the awful odor of burning flesh,

At a dinner for the Bob Hope USO, with former President Gerald Ford, and General Omar Bradley.

could ever deserve that description. He was labeled a hawk. Hope shot back that he'd rather be considered a hawk any day than a "pigeon." He even offered to help raise $10 million to help ransom captured American soldiers.

It's worth noting, too, that not everyone was criticizing Hope. For a few, the shows and the jokes were secondary to the simple fact that Hope was there in Vietnam, a living sign that the outside world still existed as they remembered it . . . that it still cared. "Bob Hope isn't really my kind of entertainer," said one soldier. "I mean, I like Red Foxx's humor better. But still, Hope's the guy who gets these people over here and no matter what you think of him, you still have to admire the guy for going out of his way for us. I know I do."

He and millions more.

REFLECTIONS

CHAPTER 4 ●

EVERY MORNING, BEFORE the sun rises, Bob Hope takes a walk. It doesn't matter what city he's in or what the new day's agenda will bring. Hope walks. Sometimes he has company, at other times he's alone.

Only Hope and God know what he thinks about on those predawn wanderings. But one thing's certain. After well over sixty years in the business of making people laugh, Hope has quite a lot to think about. Maybe he muses on Crosby, on the day's agenda or on a soldier he met somewhere, sometime, during some war.

Or, just as possibly, maybe he finally turns the great joke machine off and allows it to rest and recharge for yet another day's activities. For Bob Hope, it seems, life is just that thing God provided to feed the joke machine; there's very little in life that Hope cannot fit a quip to.

Those quips, of course, are legendary in their sheer volume. Hope has told millions of jokes in his career, and he's said to have an encyclopedic memory where they are concerned. Should that memory ever fail, Hope also has several cabinets full of neatly filed jokes, along with an index to them.

But Hope's reliance on the one-liner seems like more than habit or the frugality of a man using up already paid for merchandise. He seems not to want

the public's knowledge of him to go beyond a certain point and, in those instances, a well-timed one-liner serves as defense as much as anything else.

There are some things, though, that cannot be wisecracked around. Like the fact that Hope's years in the limelight have had their cost. Maybe some mornings as he walks the streets, the comic thinks of the years he's spent away from his wife and family.

All four of Bob Hope's children were adopted in infancy. The first was Linda, who joined the family in the summer of 1939. One year after that, the Hopes adopted another child, a boy Dolores named Tony. In 1946 Hope rounded out his family by adopting two more children, William Kelly and Nora.

Although he passed the age of eighty without looking back some time ago, the fact is that Hope tours more than most rock stars. He always has. Thus the Hope children rarely saw their father at all during their formative years.

Hope is fond of joking that he got home so infrequently that when he did go home once, the kids thought that he had been booked there. Or, he will say that when he did get home, the kids thought he was a meter reader from the utility company. "It's been suggested that I travel a bit," said Hope in one wartime routine, "that I wander from my

happy home. This is not true. Just the other evening I said to my wife, 'Dolores'—I knew it was Dolores, she introduced herself to me—'I've done an awful lot of traveling but you've been very understanding about it, although you did rent out my room.' "

When Hope moves beyond those quips to deal seriously with his role as absentee father, he credits Dolores for seeing to it that the children suffered no apparent scars because of his life-style. "My wife kept that in good perspective. She did a great job of raising our kids and I was sort of . . . a casual visitor. But they were always happy to see me. The kids never went into a sad note about the thing because we always had a lot of fun."

Daughter Linda recalls, though, that it wasn't always easy to have to share her dad with the world. "I missed him very much," she said once. "I was so sorry that he wasn't there when I was growing up. I sometimes felt angry that he wasn't there at the things other kids' fathers were present for. I felt so disappointed that he was not able to be at my high school graduation. I really wished he could have been there."

According to Linda, the people who professed to being her friends when she was in school were actually more interested in wangling an invitation to meet her famous father. She says, however, that when Hope did spend time with her and her siblings, that time belonged to *them* and he focused on what was on *their* minds.

Much of Hope's time at home—his "off" time—was actually spent in going over new material for his next appearance, film or radio show. Sometimes the kids would be allowed to feed him lines or help him act out a routine.

Linda says, "We coached him at breakfast with his lines and listened to all his jokes. He would leave doing a soft-shoe number on the porch. At dinner he would throw his voice and do a falsetto to 'Bessie, The Little Orphan Girl.' Even when we were older and knew there was no Bessie behind the curtain, we loved watching him.

"As I get older, I really appreciate that he's not your average father. It's true he was always away, but he was also there giving support when you really needed him—like when I was married and

(left) On a nostalgic visit to the house in London, where he was born. (above) Dining out in Hollywood.

divorced, for example."

Watching over all of this through the years has been the former Dolores Reade. Hope never fails to note the sacrifices she has had to make in order that he might do the work that is his life's blood. She was, after all, a popular singer in her own right when she and Hope met but, after they married, she retired. And she, like her children, has also had to get used to the fact that being Bob Hope means traveling a lot. Dolores is a devout Catholic and, although her husband doesn't share her enthusiasm, he does respect it by attending Mass at Christmas.

Dolores has accepted life as Mrs. Bob Hope with stunning grace. "I knew," she has said, "when I married him I'd have to share him with the world. My husband needs audiences like babies need milk."

According to Linda, Dolores and Bob Hope didn't make it to their half-century marriage without their share of rough spots. "It was hard for her when he went off surrounded by beautiful women. But she had made a commitment to a situation. There was always the possibility of divorce. They didn't."

One early sticking point between the couple had less to do with Hope's playboy reputation than with

Bobs daughter Linda.

entertaining the troops, his wife and children would be at home in North Hollywood, celebrating the occasion without him. In fact, the family would have to celebrate twice—once at Christmas and once a few weeks later when Hope returned. "I was twelve," quipped Linda once, "before I learned that he wasn't an airline pilot."

Hope has said that when his children became old enough, he would take them with him—to a show, a studio or a veteran's hospital, and they would begin to understand what it was he did for a living. That is, perhaps, the origin of a widely reported and amusing conversation that was overheard between Hope's children Kelly and Nora when they were little ones. William Kelly reportedly asked his sister, "Is everybody in the world Catholic?" To which Nora replied, "Everybody but Daddy. He's a comedian."

And certainly, no child ever had a simpler, more direct and more accurate understanding of what motivates her pop. Hope has tried in other ways to bring his family closer to his professional life. Daughter Linda came aboard as a producer at Hope Enterprises, the comedian's company. And although she retired years ago, Dolores still sings with and for her husband on special occasions. One such occasion was an NBC birthday tribute that took place on board a U.S. aircraft carrier.

One thing Dolores stopped doing with her husband back in the '60s was playing golf. She insisted that he welched on a dollar bet after losing the game to her.

Hope has often said that show business is just what he does between golf games and, indeed, he is almost as well known for golf as he is for his ski nose and trip-hammer monologues. The comic was first introduced to the game during his days as a caddie and it was evidently love at first putt.

By one account, Hope pays over $40,000 a year to country clubs across the country to maintain his memberships. His Toluca Lake estate had the aforementioned golf course built in to it. On the greens, Hope the easygoing guy reportedly turns into Hope the merciless. He is a serious competitor.

According to Jackie Gleason, "Bob's only departure from sanity is his insistence that he can beat me." On the ninth hole of a charity game in Florida

Dolores's desire for a home. Hope, who preferred renting and leasing to the concrete permanence of a mortgage, resisted her suggestions for years. Dolores persevered and, eventually, the couple bought a home in the Toluca Lake neighborhood of North Hollywood. The fifteen-room mansion houses Hope's library and office, and the estate also includes a golf course and swimming pool. The remodeling was done during one of Hope's extended absences and he says that when he returned, "I let Dolores guide me to my own room so I would know I was home. I was sharp enough to leave strict orders about the Captain's Cabin. Not one piece of dust was ever to be shifted."

Indeed, Hope's bedroom is described jokingly as the one room in his home where "the maid fears to tread." Hope prefers to conduct business, when he is at home, from the telephone in his bedroom.

Hope's holdings also include a mammoth, multi-million-dollar Palm Springs estate built along a futuristic design. As it turned out, that project was fraught with unexpected danger. Perhaps the most publicized incident was when a stray spark from a welder's torch ignited a blaze that burned the house to the ground.

During the holiday seasons Hope spent abroad

44

(below) Riding on the Golf Course. (right) Buddy Hackett dropped by to say Hello to Bob and Dyan Cannon, while they were taping a show for NBC.

between the two men, Hope watched three of his shots sink into the water. "He kept expecting me to say something," Gleason said, "but I just sat there serenely puffing on a cigarette. When he finally got over the water, I just said, 'Nice shot.' It killed him."

"Sometimes," said Hope once, "I think my real racket is golf. The other things I do are just sidelines." Bing Crosby, a man who knew about such things, once said that, when it comes to golf, Hope is a man you'd rather have with you than against you.

To satisfy his love for golf, Hope makes sure to play the game at least once a day, often rising early and squeezing in a few holes before getting on with the business of the day. In addition, he sponsors the Bob Hope Desert Golf classic. His adversaries on the green are many and famous. Besides Crosby and Gleason, they have also included a prominent politician or two—like former presidents Carter, Ford, and Nixon, along with former vice-president Spiro

46

(below)In Vegas with Totie Fields. (right) With old friend Bing Crosby. (far right above) Hope and Crosby with the girls. (far right below)With wife Dolores when he received the Entertainer of the Year award.

Agnew. Hope once quipped that the biggest misconception about him is that he's a good golfer.

Hope says he has also labored under another "misconception." That misconception has to do with his wealth, which has been estimated by *Fortune, Forbes* and *Time* magazines at figures he has often called wildly exaggerated. Those estimates rank him as the richest entertainer in Hollywood and one of the wealthiest men in the United States; he has been reported to have as much as an incredible $750

million dollars.

"*Fortune* put me right up there with J. Paul Getty and Doris Duke," said Hope once. "Why, I couldn't even be a bellboy for those guys." He insists that he is not worth $200 million, let alone the more astronomical $750 million. If he had the money he is reputed to have, Hope once cracked, he wouldn't go to Vietnam. He'd send for it. When the editors of one magazine riled him with an estimate he considered exaggerated, Hope wired them. "You find

50

(previous page) The Mike Douglas Show salutes Bob Hope, and got the old USO gang together again.

it and I'll split it."

In the end, Hope's wealth is rightfully a matter between him, his accountants and his checkbook. But it's safe to say that, whatever he's worth, Hope is set for life. The comedian, who likes to joke that he has to keep working because his tax payments are running the government, doesn't ever have to work again if he doesn't wish to. That's the bottom line. And Hope knows he has it good. The best thing about having money, he once said, is not hav-

ing to look at the right-hand side of the menu.

The comedian reportedly amassed his fortune on the strength of some surprisingly shrewd and fortuitous investments and business maneuvers that went through, not at the suggestion of some business manager, but because of decisions made by Hope himself. A business manager looking for a job with Hope is said to have approached the comic's banker once and asked him to slip in a good word. The banker replied that, on the strength of what he

51

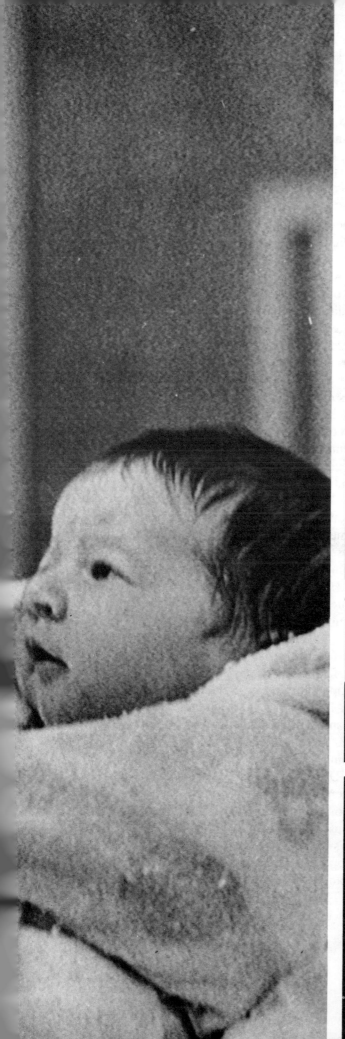

(left) Bob became a Grandfather for the fourth time, when daughter Nora gave birth to a girl in San Francisco. (below) With Phyllis Diller and Johnny Carson. (middle) Lets get down to business. (bottom) A rare night out with Dolores.

(left) Alan King, Bob Hope, George Burns, and seated Red Buttons.
(left below) With Jack Benny (right) George Burns, Ann Margaret and Bob share a laugh. (right below) Bob with Cary Grant.

had seen Hope do with money, perhaps the business manager should try to hire Hope to oversee *his* funds.

Hope says his wealth grew out of keeping up with the Crosbys. "In 1937 I went out to join Bing Crosby at Paramount. He had a big house in the valley, so I bought a big house. He bought a limo and I bought a limo. Then, in 1949, Bing and I got lucky in oil. The stock market was down so I bought land."

Actually, Hope bought a *lot* of land, becoming in the process the biggest single property owner in California. One of his shrewdest investments is reputed to be his purchase of 16,000 acres of the San Fernando Valley at a time when the area was all farmland. Hope paid something like $40 an acre. Developers gave Hope a fantastic return on that investment in later years, turning such San Fernando Valley communities as Northridge, Encino and Woodland Hills into popular shopping and residential centers. Similarly, when Hope and Crosby bought into oil in 1949 they were lucky enough to find themselves a gusher.

Hope's holdings are not limited to oil and land, though, and they're not all in California. At one time or another, the comedian has also bought into baseball's Cleveland Indians, RCA and a soft drink company.

Hope's attitude toward cash has always been a touch idiosyncratic as well. Despite his alleged stinginess, the comic gives thousands of dollars a year to charity. He also gives thousands of hours, performing at benefits and at charity golf games.

Though he is one of the wealthiest of Americans, Hope's impoverished childhood has still left its mark on him. It's as if, behind the quips, he still has a desperate fear of being poor. "I can't just sit back and play golf," he told *People*. "I want to keep going."

Driven by this desire to "keep going," Hope has been a tireless pitchman for such sponsors as Texaco, California Federal Savings and Diet Coke because, as he puts it, he needs the money. Apparently he's worth the money, too. Texaco has said that Hope has given it a higher profile with consumers than the company ever had before.

Though he routinely denies as exaggerated the assessments of his worth made by the magazines,

54

(right) With Mitzi Gaynor (middle) Former President Gerald Ford with Carol Burnett and Bob Hope, holding their "People's Choice" awards. (below) Bing Crosby, Dorothy Lamour, Bob Hope and Debbie Reynolds (next page) Hold on a moment Sugar Ray Robinson, let me catch my pants.

Hope does freely admit that: "I am rich. My God, anybody that has the kind of money I have is rich, the kind of prospects I have."

One of Hope's biggest yearly expenditures is his writing staff's salaries, which reported run well into the hundreds of thousands of dollars. Hope's writers, often described as the best in the business, work hard for that money, too, grinding out the gags for a boss who expects them to be always on call and always quick with the quips. At the rapid-fire pace Hope uses up those jokes, quick is the only way to be.

Hope has always seemed to expect of his writers nothing less than that he be top priority in their lives. That expectation has led to some amusing and telling situations over the years. Like the time one writer asked him for time off to honeymoon during the making of a movie. Hope is reported to have offered the writer an entire afternoon.

The comic has been known to wake his writers in the middle of the night with a phone call seeking appropriate material for a situation in which he had found himself. He once flew his entire team to Europe at a moment's notice. The writers once coined an acronym (NAFT, which stands for Need A Few Things) to describe Hope's calls.

There was, for instance, the time Hope was touring military installations and noticed that his plane was going to land on grass. He asked his writers for some instant grass runway quips and they delivered.

Al Boasberg was the first of the many writers hired by Hope. He was responsible for such Hope gems as:

"My brother slapped Al Capone once."

"Why, he's the bravest man I ever heard of. I'd like to shake his hand."

"We couldn't dig him up just for that."

No one doubts that Hope could write his own material. In fact, he has often been described as a most accomplished student of joke structure. In preparing for a major show, he has been known to order his writers to cook up much more material than he will be able to use. He then sifts through it, tries it out and, eventually, cuts it down to a fast-paced monologue that breezes almost effortlessly from big laugh to big laugh.

The jokes that don't make the show, though, are

(insets) Sharing a joke with Don Rickles.

not thrown away. They are instead saved in Hope's joke file for future reference. Hope also has his advance men research the characteristics of any town or military base in which he will be playing. When that research comes back, the writing staff is able to construct a personalized monologue, complete with localized references. "Anything local like that," says Hope, "they know you've thought about them, about their scene."

Since Hope has shown himself to be a very talented joke writer, there is something a little inscrutable in his reported insistence that his writing staff be on call at all times. Perhaps, even after all these years, he's still just a bit worried about the idea of not having precisely the right thing to say at the right time.

One former Hope writer told *TV Guide,* "We used to have to hang around outside the taping room (when Hope was doing a TV special) so he could see us. We called it 'registering on the emulsion.' Hope wanted to know we cared."

Like the Boy Scouts, Hope enjoys being prepared. "I'm such a ham" he told one writer. "Somebody said if I was in a blizzard and two Eskimo dogs walked by, I'd do ten minutes for them. But I'm not the kind of a guy who's on all the time either. I don't wanna be on all the time. But I can get up *anywhere* if I have to and do five to seven minutes. I will walk through a hotel lobby and a guy grabs me and says, 'Hey, be a funny guy to this lady,' so I do try."

Together with his writers, Hope has carved a comedic style that is as familiarly and comfortingly America as Mt. Rushmore or the Statue of Liberty. Hope mounts the stage with a cavalier stroll, his mouth fixed in a grin that is part leer. Behind the shining eyes, you can almost see the great joke machine humming away, making last-minute adjustments in content and timing.

When Hope starts his routine, the gags come fast—a scattershot style that requires constant attention lest the listener miss something. And if the joke is not so good, that doesn't matter. This is Bob

58

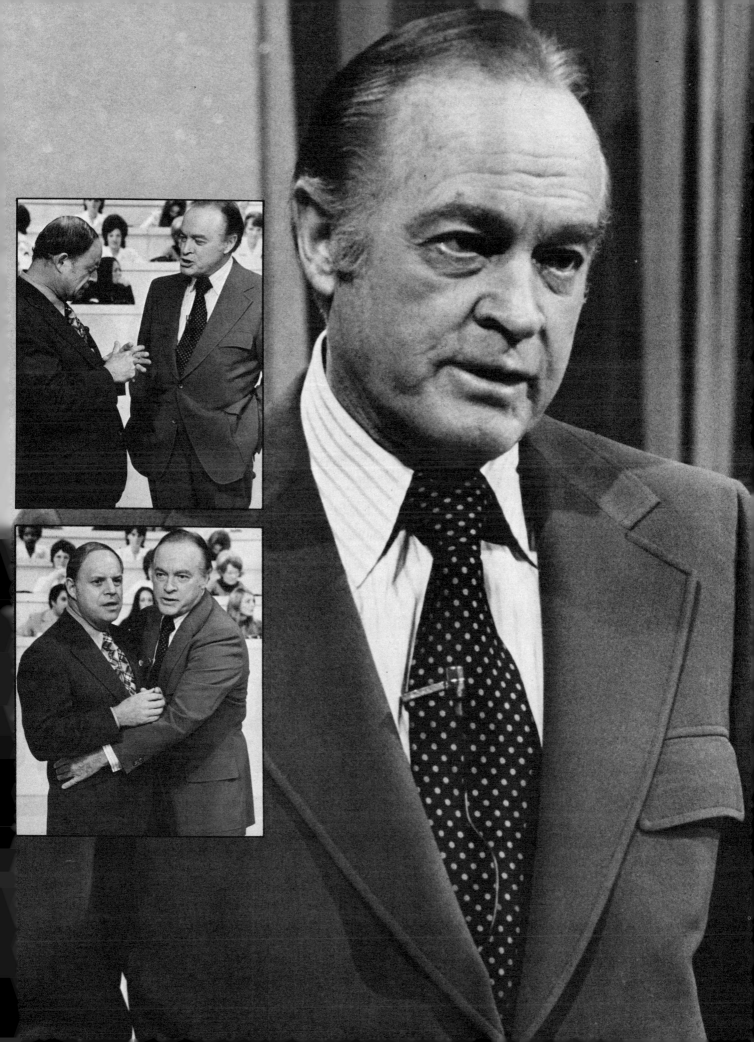

(left) Bob visits the Playboy Club (below) Laughing it up with Billy Martin, ex manager of the New York Yankees

61

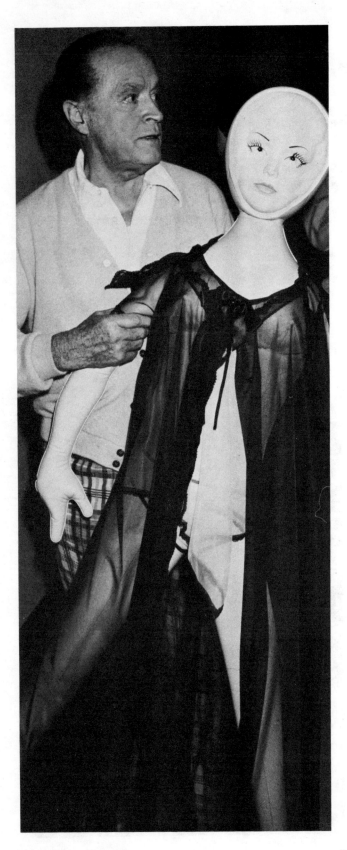

Hope. Like Johnny Carson, Hope has built a special appeal out of milking laughs from a gag that fails.

Hope has been described as "lethally neutral" because of a comedy style that plays no real favorites where subject matter is concerned. Although Hope has his taboos where material is concerned (death and heavy sex, for instance), he has no known sacred cows. He has gone after Democrat and Republican, liberal and conservative, saint and sinner alike with a wit that stops safely short of offending any of his subjects.

The only requirement for being included in a Hope monologue seems to be whether or not the subject is in the news. The key seems to be that the gag is topical. Hope once wrote, "Audiences like to see the big guy get it, not the little guy. I learned that in my early vaudeville days. I was a pretty brash kid in those days. I'd come onstage and take charge of the whole city. My attitude was that if they didn't get the joke, they were pretty dumb. But then I had an afterpiece, two guys in box seats who would start heckling me and knocking me down. And the audience loved it—loved to see the big guy getting his dignity punctured."

And of course, the big guys don't seem to mind. In fact, many of them are honored to consider Hope a friend—and even more honored when he publicly roasts them in one of his monologues. Hope's high-level friendships include cardinals, heads of state, captains of industry and every president since Franklin Delano Roosevelt. Among the countless honorary doctorates, trophies, plaques and awards he has received, Hope has a special honor bestowed upon him by one of those presidents—John Fitzgerald Kennedy—in 1963. That's the year Congress voted Hope a gold medal as "America's most prized Ambassador of Good Will."

Unlike the "timeless" humor of other funny men and women, Hope's topical brand of comedy is very much tied to time. The only constant is his timing and his refusal to offend.

In the '30s, when prevailing fashion trends caused hemlines to fall, Hope quipped that, "Long dresses don't bother me. I've got a good memory."

During the '40s, with World War II raging in Europe and Americans forced to accept food rationing, Hope joked that, "This year in Hollywood, I

62

Bob was named an honorary member of the Harlem Globe Trotteers

saw a crowd of civilians going crazy. They were gathered outside of the post office and the president of the ration board was leaning out of the window with a T-bone steak on a yo-yo."

On one wartime military tour, Hope zinged the British with the observation that "Churchill certainly travels; he's been in Casablanca more than Humphrey Bogart." While President Roosevelt had his running feud with the *Chicago Tribune*, Hope joked that FDR's dog, Fala, was the only pooch "to be housebroken on the *Chicago Tribune*."

The '50s, and Senator Joseph McCarthy's rabid anti-Communist campaign, moved Hope to claim that he had it "on good authority that Senator Joe McCarthy is going to disclose the names of two million Communists. He just got his hands on a Moscow telephone book."

The '60s, that decade of turbulence and confusion, brought with it a wealth of material that Hope seemingly just ripped right out of the front page of the morning paper. Hope told GIs he had "good news" for them: "The country is behind you—50%." Then-California governor Ronald Reagan, according to Hope, had "a secret plan to win the war. He will release it just as soon as John Wayne finishes his picture."

In the '70s, Hope also enjoyed joking about the celebrated klutziness of former President Gerald Ford. "I played golf with Jerry just the other day," he would say. "He got a birdie, an eagle, an elk, a moose and a Mason."

"Has comedy changed over the years?" asked Hope in print. "Yes and no. The basics are still there, but there is more permissiveness today. There's been," said Hope, "a complete flip-flop in what you can and can't do. In vaudeville we did a lot of ethnic comedy—Polish jokes, Irish jokes, jokes about blacks, Indians, Jews . . . 'Amos 'n' Andy' was a masterpiece of black character comedy. But try an ethnic joke today and you get a letter from some foreign embassy. Tell a black joke and you're suddenly a racist."

The fact is that Hope's audience knows him. They know his subject matter and his style. They

65

know that his targets will survive unhurt and that they will be, in any case, himself and other "big guys" who can take it. All that remains is for them to see how Hope puts it all together. As one Hope booster put it, the fans start laughing the moment they buy the ticket.

Who is Bob Hope anyway? Dolores Hope, who should know better than anybody, once said that she sometimes has trouble reading her husband of half a century, that he is such a cheerful person by nature that she can't always tell when he's upset about something. "I'm an up person," agrees Hope. "I don't worry too much. But sometimes, just before dawn, I wake up and I lie there thinking about things . . ."

Although he has largely escaped the ravages of time, Hope is not immortal. And, as time has changed his material and the way we look at it, so, too, has time changed the man himself. His hair has thinned, he has age spots and a heart problem (it was pumping too fast) once caused some concern. In addition, Hope has had recurring problems with hemorrhaging of the eyes.

But overall the man is in remarkably good health and has the stamina and energy of people half his age. Which is a good thing because he apparently intends to go on forever, barely slackening his pace to acknowledge the fact that he is getting older. Around Hope "retirement" is a dirty word.

Retire?

"That would be dumb and dull."

Retire?

"So many people in our business are so *sick* from having quit. I would have to hire an applause machine just to get me up in the morning if I retired."

Retire? No way.

"Why should I stop? What fun is that? What would I do if I stopped? Play golf? I do that now. When people sit back and say, 'Well, I've had it,' they have. I haven't."

Hope has been asked about retirement so often that he characteristically has the answers ready and waiting before the first syllables are out of the questioner's mouth. The bottom line seems to be that he *won't* retire, unless forced to do so by some infirmity. And therein lies some clue to the "real" Bob Hope. He is, as one observer put it, exactly what he

seems to be—no more and no less. What you see on the *Tonight Show is* Bob Hope. He is, apparently, miraculously free of the unique schizophrenia of most star performers—wherein their public and private personas are worlds apart. And thus comedy is not something Hope does. It is, rather, something he *is.* Take that away from him and you take away part of the man. His comedy is his tonic.

There are several examples that illustrate that point. For instance, there's the time in 1963 that eye surgery forced Hope to miss the first leg of his annual Christmas tour of military installations. As soon as he was able, the comic joined his troupe in Turkey. "He looked like a sick man," one of his assistants told *Time,* "but when he walked on the stage, the roar that went up from those people was probably the world's greatest therapy. From that moment on, you could physically see the change. He was his old self, rarin' to go."

"I enjoy entertaining," says Hope. "Enjoy being around an audience that laughs. It's excitement and that's the key word in life. That's the whole bit in life."

Hope says, "Laughter opens up the arteries. I tell people to keep that in mind the rest of the show. And I get a lot of therapy out of it myself. There's nothing like doing your work well, and you like to practice your art with an audience."

Fortunately, he has managed to remain very much in demand for audiences. Those crowds may be a bit older now than they once were, but that doesn't matter. What's important is that they still turn out in droves for him.

And within the entertainment community itself, Hope is similarly popular. *Time* found that out by asking his peers about him. "You spell Bob Hope c-l-a-s-s-," gushed Lucille Ball. "I'd like to get the applause at the end of my show that he gets before he opens his mouth," said Joey Bishop. Woody Allen called Hope a "terrific influence on every stand-up, one-line monologist. The thing which makes him great can't be stolen or imitated." Jack Benny told *Time,* "It's not enough just to get laughs. The audience has to love you, and Bob gets love as well as laughs from his audiences." Crosby liked to say of his pal Hope, "If the light went on in the icebox, he'd start to perform." It's curious how, after all the praise from all the critics and peers, that one humorous observation may well come closest to the essential truth.

One of the most amazing things about Hope is the fact that, in over sixty years of entertaining, he has never really been out of the public's favor, never found himself at the center of some scandal. There have been times when something of that nature could have happened, though. The Vietnam controversy, for instance, could have damaged his popularity much more than it did.

But it didn't. And if so deep an emotional split couldn't knock Bob Hope from his pinnacle, revelations about his personal style and tastes barely registered a murmur from his fans. There is, for instance, the revelation that Hope once had the beginnings of a potential drinking problem.

"I used to be the king of the daiquiris," he said once. "I suppose it started here at the [Lakeside Golf] club. I'd buy a drink, then another, then another. . . . I could handle three-four drinks a night. You don't get drunk, but the stuff is, you know, *around*. So I threw up at a few people's houses. I'd send them notes: 'I fertilized your garden.' " Hope, who neither drinks nor smokes now, says he stopped the former habit because a doctor told him it would lead him to prostate, liver and bladder problems that would eventually kill him. And being dead would mean he couldn't play golf, so. . . .

In the end, balanced against everything else that Bob Hope is and has done, an almost-drinking problem doesn't amount to much, and that's because talking about it costs Hope absolutely nothing in terms of audience support.

Bob Hope is as invulnerable as an entertainer can be. If he never boards another plane, never tells another joke, his place in history is assured. In fact, it was assured long ago. He still has his goals. He has talked about jumping back into films by doing a biography of Walter Winchell, but so far, it's just talk.

There are still other goals, too. Hope wants an Oscar. He's won the statuette for his humanitarian efforts, but just once, he says he'd like to win on the strength of an actual film performance. The Emmy is another Hollywood trinket that hasn't yet made it to Bob Hope's trophy room. Surprisingly

A little birthday cake for Bob.

enough, Hope has also never played Las Vegas. He says he came close once; he was offered a record sum to play the gambling capital, but reportedly he wanted the deal arranged so that the venue would buy into some of his property. The negotiations subsequently fell through.

Again, in the end, what does any of that matter against the whole? And the whole is the simple fact that young Leslie Townes Hope of Eltham, England, grew up to be the richest funnyman in America, and the most seen, most durable comic in the world. He is a star many times over, in more media than virtually any of the latter-day stars; vaudeville, radio, Broadway, films, television and live stand-up comedy were all changed just because of his presence.

With Hope, all the hoary old clichés apply: legend, star, king of comedy, and so on. But if the prize has been great, so, too, has the price. That price has been paid, not by the "public" Bob Hope, but by the private Hope and his family. That family paid by learning to cope with his frequent extended absences. But perhaps the private Hope himself paid the greater price long ago. Whoever he was, whatever he might have become, he simply vanished to allow his public alter ego uncontested control of center stage.

Hope still remembers, doubtless with bittersweet emotion, the time he was leaving the house and one of his kids saw him off, saying, "Goodbye, Bob Hope."

And after all, that is who—and what—he is.

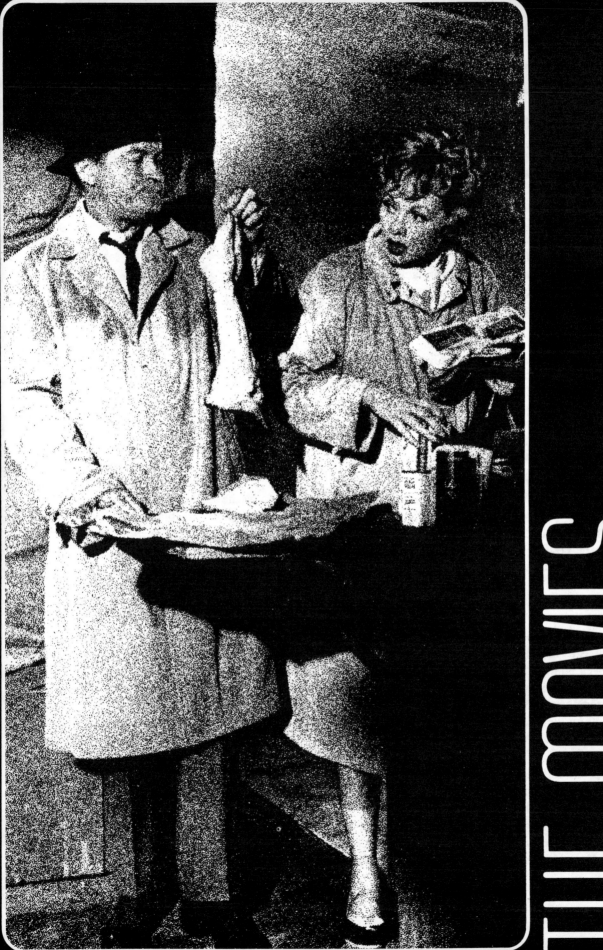

THE MOVIES

CHAPTER 5 ●

HOLLYWOOD WASN'T HOLDING its breath waiting on Bob Hope to arrive.

The comedian, bereft of audience feedback, had come off unforgivably stiff and square-jawed in his earlier screen test. Hope hadn't liked Hollywood and Hollywood hadn't liked him, and for the next few years that was pretty much that.

It was a stroke of luck and timing that finally brought Hope and Hollywood together for what would turn out in the end to be a lasting relationship. It was 1938 and Paramount was putting together a musical revue called *The Big Broadcast of 1938*. Jack Benny's name had been thrown as a top candidate for the role of Buzz Fielding, master of ceremonies. But Benny wasn't available. Remembering Hope from a Broadway show, the producers and director of *The Big Broadcast* decided that he would fit the vacant spot rather neatly and Hope agreed.

The movie included such Paramount contract players as W. C. Fields, Martha Raye, Shirley Ross, Lynn Overman and Ben Blue. It also reteamed Hope with two of his radio cohorts, Patricia "Honey Chile" Walker and singer Dorothy Lamour.

In the film, Ross was Hope's wife in a deteriorating marriage which eventually wound up in the divorce court. A chance meeting on a trans-Atlantic liner and a few drinks later, the two make up with

a song, which caught the fancy of millions, including columnist Damon Runyon. "What a delivery," he gushed in his column, "what a song, what an audience reception."

What a song, indeed. "Thanks For The Memory" went on to become Hope's signature tune. Hardly anyone recalls the original lyrics by now; they've been made over and cornballed up many times to suit whatever skit or routine Hope might have been in the middle of at the time. But in the end those four words mean Bob Hope, no matter what the lyric that frames them.

"Thanks For The Memory" was one of the very few worthwhile things (besides money) that Hope got out of his first feature film role. Unlike the roles Hope found himself in in later films, the character of "Buzz" Fielding was not a wisecracking comic. He was the straight man to the low comedy of W. C. Fields and, in another sense, very similar to the sort of characters Hope had played on Broadway.

Still, if *Broadcast* wasn't a landmark, it was, at least, a start. Later, Hope would refine and more fully develop the comic persona that was to carry him through the decades. Excluding the short films he made early on in his career, the following is a complete filmography of Hope's thirty-four years of movie magic:

College Swing (1938)—Despite the glowing

praise from Runyon, Paramount didn't seem too impressed with Hope, dropping him into a minor role in this "B" movie produced by Lewis Gensler. The film featured Hope as Bud "Studyhard" Brady, helping a girl (Gracie Allen) pass her college entrance test. After a little talk with Gensler, who also remembered Hope from their days together with the production of Broadway's *Ballyhoo,* the comedian was able to wangle himself a bigger role, but it didn't really make a difference.

Give Me A Sailor (1938)—Hope was navy officer Jim Brewster, a man in love, in a comedy that also featured Nana Bryant, Edward Earle, Betty Grable, Clarence Kolb, Kathleen Lockhart and Martha Raye;

Thanks For The Memory (1938)—Paramount was obviously inspired by the runaway success of the earlier song of the same name when they dished this one up. *Thanks* was another marriage-on-the-rocks-saved-by-a-song film—with Hope playing a novelist and working alongside such performers as Eddie "Rochester" Anderson, Charles Butterworth, William Collier, Hedda Hopper, Jack Norton, Shirley Ross and Honey Chile Wilder;

Never Say Die (1938)—Hope was a rich hypochondriac in this slapstick, which also featured Martha Raye, Andy Devine and Paul Harvey;

Some Like It Hot (1939)—This movie broadened Hope's exposure to film and set him up for his next role, which was to prove another major stepping-stone in his screen career. In *Hot,* Hope was a crazy concessionaire, clowning with a host of Paramount players including Wayne "Tiny" Whitt, Clarence H. Wilson and Una Merkel;

The Cat And The Canary (1938)—In this film, Hope was Wally Hampton, a mystery-story buff who suddenly finds himself smack in the middle of a real life thriller. Paulette Goddard was a young heiress who is convinced her life is in danger. Hope is the only one who believes her tale, so he decides to help her;

Cat also included John Beal, Douglass Montgomery, Elizabeth Patterson, Willard Robertson, Gale Sondergaard, and George Zucco. The film was based on the mystery-melodrama play by John Willard, and was brought to the screen by screenwriters Walter De Leon and Lynn Starling as a horror comedy.

The Wally Hampton role was the first to allow Hope to really develop as a film comic with a style and wit all his own. In one scene for example, Hope is asked, "Don't big empty houses scare you?" "Not me," quips Hope, "I used to be in vaudeville." This tendency to resort to quips, particularly in dangerous situations, is a characteristic that was to appear repeatedly in Hope's films—particularly in the "Road" series.

In another scene, Hope displayed an early bent toward a later trademark—the topical joke. He is asked, "Do you believe in reincarnation . . . you know, that dead people always come back?" "You mean like the Republicans?" he asks.

Then there was the odd little habit Hope began to display of turning from cowardly chump into unwilling hero. *Cat* also brought to light Hope's ever-present desire to be a lady's man. He tells Goddard, "My mother brought me up never to be caught twice in the same lady's bedroom."

Overall, *Cat* was a very important launching base for Hope. It was a critical and popular success and probably played a very important role in convincing Paramount that Hope could be a big box office draw after all.

THE ROADS—

The Road To Singapore (1940)—Another milestone in Hope's career. It marked the first time he, Bing Crosby and Dorothy Lamour worked together in front of a camera. It also set the stage for a seven-part series of films that would forever brand Hope a lovably silly, uniquely American and eternally cowardly hero.

But Hope and his costars almost didn't get the chance to create these legendary "Road" movies, because they were not exactly the team Paramount had in mind when casting the films began. The studio had originally hoped to snare George Burns and Gracie Allen, but their schedules prevented them from accepting the parts.

Next, Paramount tried to get Fred MacMurray and Jack Oakie for the male leads but, once again, there were problems. Finally the studio, probably throwing up its corporate hands in despair, settled on the untried team of Crosby and Hope.

In *The Road To Singapore* Hope played Ace

Lannigan, an itinerant who hops a boat to the Far East with his friend Crosby, who played the son of a rich shipping tycoon. In the Orient, the two meet a lovely native girl (Lamour) who flips for Crosby, setting a pattern that was to leave audiences howling and Hope frustrated through most of the succeeding "Road" pictures.

In *Singapore,* Lamour doesn't consider herself good enough for her chosen mate, and Crosby's father doesn't do anything to change her mind on that score. Lamour ends up settling for Hope, later realizing that it's really Crosby she wants. Hope gallantly, albeit reluctantly, steps aside.

The plot of *Singapore* (a film which was originally called *The Road To Mandalay*) is rather sketchy and undeveloped, and paradoxically, therein lies its charm. The loose script provides numerous opportunities for Hope and Crosby to get into and out of a series of bruising scrapes.

Although not as pronounced here as in later "Road" films, *Singapore* also provided a forum for the running feud between Hope and Crosby. As one critic put it, the aim of the pictures always seemed to be for the two old pros to see who could step on the other's lines to best effect. Although the names of the characters were changed to protect the innocent, Hope and Crosby essentially played Hope and Crosby (their public images that is) throughout the "Road" series, forever attempting to upstage one another and with Hope occasionally tissing witty asides to the audience.

Measured side by side, the characters that Hope and Crosby played were total opposites. Hope was an overanxious, overeager, brash and bumbling loverboy, using endless chatter to convince others and himself that he is in charge. Crosby, on the other hand, is the cool, suave, debonair type, chivalrous to a fault and always ready to aid a damsel in distress.

Yet for all their differences, the pair also had common ground between them. Marriage for both was a four-letter word. Violence was also something to be studiously avoided, as there was too much danger one of the guys could get hurt.

Despite its lack of a solid plot, *Singapore* was a box office success, prompting the studio to crank out a second "Road" picture—1941's *The Road*

To Zanzibar. Like its predecessor, *Zanzibar* was originally written as a serious picture, this time about two men stranded in the jungles of Madagascar. However, *Stanley and Livingston* was then a current film and, because of the potential for similarity between the two films, it was decided that Paramount's film would have to be reworked.

Already, the "Road" formula of running over the barebones plot with ad lib after ad lib was pretty much set. "We'd go to the set," Hope says, "and the stage hands were waiting for us to do nutty stuff. We wouldn't disappoint them. We'd come up with something. The crew recognizes something different. The crew recognizes a hit."

Although the Crosby-Hope chemistry was popular with crew, critics and ticket holders, the duo's writers were often less pleased to see their precious prose treated so cavalierly. Hope recalled that, "After *Zanzibar* won the National Board of Review Award, some guys interviewed us and then they said, 'Yeah, they ad lib a lot on the set.' And Don Hartman, he didn't like that, because he and Butler (Frank) had written a hell of a script. So we walked on the set one day and I yelled, 'If you hear one of your lines, yell bingo!' Oh, that burned him up. He went back to the office and he screamed . . . And the guy said, 'Yeah, look at the grosses—and your name is right out there in big type.' "

"So pretty soon all that hostility was gone and he started smiling. I loved that guy, thought he was a great fellow. But it's what *made* the pictures, those extra touches. And the audience was in on it. They knew that we were fooling around." At the box office, *Zanzibar* "fooled around" to the tune of a 1.5 million dollar gate. *Morocco* was next in 1942.

The plot was simple enough. The boys started out broke and Crosby, ever the suave hustler, decided to alleviate the situation (for himself, at least), by selling his "buddy" into slavery. The "slavery" Hope finds, however, is something to be envied—not pitied. He luxuriates under the tender ministrations of Dorothy Lamour, blissfully unaware that he is being set up to take a big fall . . . a marriage designed to fill a prophesy.

Crosby, meanwhile, has had a change of heart— a change influenced by Hope's Aunt Lucy (Hope), who berates him for what he's done to her nephew.

Crosby arrives on the scene in time to save Hope from the terrors of the altar; Lamour falls for Crosby, handmaiden Dona Drake swoons for Hope, and the four flee an outraged Anthony Quinn.

Critical reaction to *The Road to Morocco* was mixed. The *New York Times* called the movie a "lampoon of all pictures having to do with exotic romance, played by a couple of wise guys who can make a gag do everything but lay an egg."

The *Herald-Tribune,* however, was less impressed. That paper's critic accused Paramount of "teetering on the edge of antic vulgarity" in the Hope-Crosby films, and of taking a "nose dive" with Morocco.

Unfortunately for the *Tribune, Morocco* was another smash with the only critics who really count —the public. It would be three more years before the series picked up again.

The Road To Utopia was next, and it marked several important changes. Chief among those changes was the fact that "Road" writer Don Hartman was no longer on the team. Although his erstwhile partner, Frank Butler, was still a "roadie," Hope had by this time brought his own gag writers aboard as well.

"I would give them the script," he has said, "that they would bring the jokes in and I would edit them and call Bing into my room and say, 'What do you think of this? What do you think of that?' "

Hope has often called his gag team the best in the world, but many Road fans felt that *Utopia* was not up to the exacting standards of hilarity that had been set by *Morocco.* For one thing, in yet another departure from form, this picture was set in no-far-away-land of mystery and intrigue, but in Alaska.

Once again, Hope and Crosby are flat broke, having lost their money after Hope mistakes a ship's porthole for a safe and tosses the loot in. It seems that the *Road to Utopia* finds Hope the victim of other comic misunderstandings as well—like the

scene in which he goes into a clinch with a grizzly bear that he thinks is Dorothy in furs.

Utopia introduced humorist Robert Benchley as a narrator. Unfortunately, many people reported finding him more a distraction from the plot than a help. Finally, *Utopia* strayed from the familiar *Road* formula in one more very important way. In this one, Hope finally gets the girl—or does he?

You're left to make up your own mind when the camera takes us back to visit the happy (?) couple twenty years later, as they are visited by Crosby. After spending a little time reminiscing about adventures past, the trio turn to talking about Hope and Crosby's son. At which point the camera happens to pick out a photo of the young fella—and he's the spitting image of Crosby.

After another three years had lapsed, Hope and Crosby hit the road again. Destination? *Rio.* In this one, Hope is "Hot Lips" Barton, a trumpeter paired with a singing partner (Crosby) who seemingly can't resist giving aid, succor, and all the duo's hard-earned cash to every distressed damsel that he meets.

In an effort to make some quick cash, Crosby shanghais Hope into bicycling across a high wire; the stunt fails and the two are forced to run for their lives with a bilked circus owner and his boys in hot pursuit. They end up stowing away on a boat to Rio (Hope carried aboard by Crosby masquerading as a side of beef). Naturally, they soon encounter Lamour, who is a distressed young heiress being forced into a loveless marriage of convenience by an "aunt."

Rio also featured the Andrews Sisters, who team with Crosby on a peppy number called "You Don't Have To Know The Language." Crosby and the ladies show off a little fancy stepping while Hope is limited to blowing his horn from the bandstand.

A little further down this particular *Road,* Hope and Crosby show up in disguise at Lamour's wedding, determined to save her. Of course, they first have to save themselves from the clutches of her "aunt" and her extermination-minded henchmen.

The two wind up decked out as Latin dancers performing for the wedding party. Their wild dance takes them all over the courtyard, cavorting daringly close to the henchmen who sit there nonchalantly, apparently completely taken in by the ruse.

Part of the charm of the dance is the anticipation that, any minute, things will go wrong and Hope and Crosby will be on the lam once again. Certainly their disguises have been put together in such slapdash haste that you almost expect the fruit-bowl

In the end, of course, the hero (Hope, this time) walks into the sunset with the girl. It's only later that a mystified Crosby finds out the reason his ski-nosed chum has been able to pull off this particular trick—hypnotism.

Nineteen fifty-three saw the release of the next *Road* picture, *Bali*. Hope was Harold Gridley, a vaudeville song-and-dance man on the run with his partner, Crosby. The two wind up stranded on a beautiful tropical island where Lamour (as Princess

"Road To Utopia" with Dorothy Lamour and Bing Crosby.

hat perched on Hope's head to fly off. But it never does.

That isn't to say, though, that the boys get away with the game. They end up giving themselves away when, instead of dancing their way out of the courtyard, they wind up flinging themselves into the laps of their would-be assassins.

Lalah) reigns. The heavy this time out is an evil prince out to nab the proverbial sunken treasure. *Bali* featured a host of guest stars, including Humphrey Bogart, Jane Russell, Dean Martin and Jerry Lewis.

The famous trio finally came to the end of their *Road* series in 1962 with *The Road To Hong Kong*.

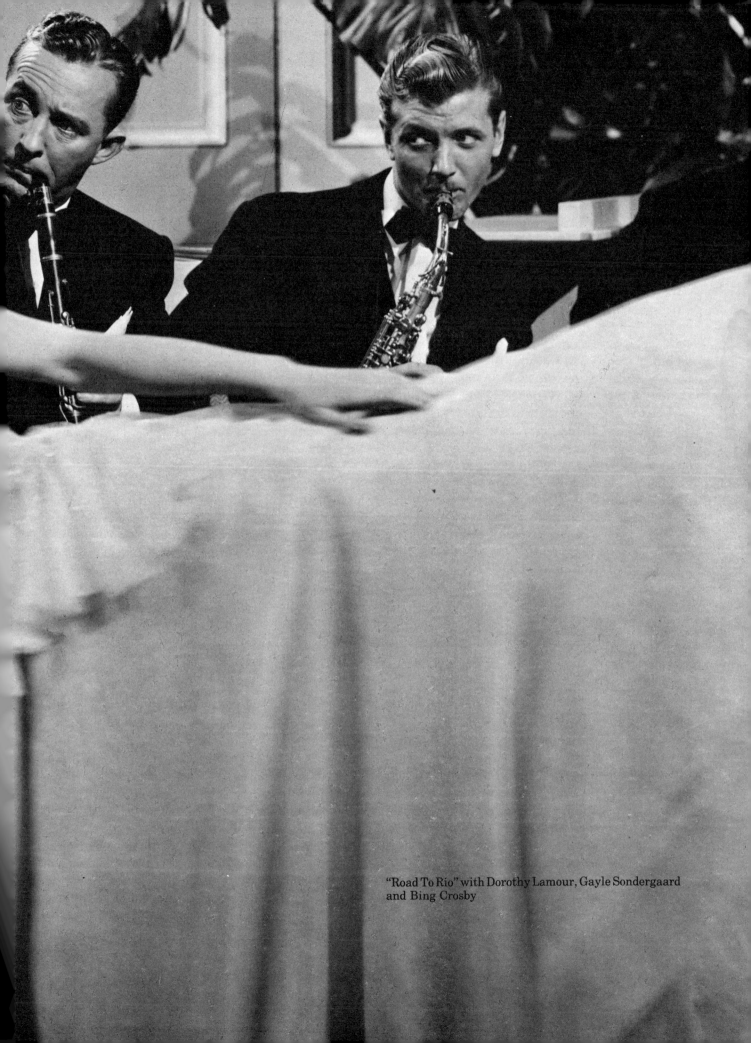

"Road To Rio" with Dorothy Lamour, Gayle Sondergaard and Bing Crosby

Critics agreed almost universally that, by this time, the magic of the *Road* series had been stretched thin. Interestingly enough, Lamour wasn't allowed to play the love interest in this final trip down the *Road* (she was deemed too old, despite being younger than both principals), although she did make an appearance. Her traditional role was filled by young Joan Collins, who would later come to fame in television's *Dynasty*.

Twenty-two years and seven *Roads* later, the premise had run out of steam—or, perhaps, its two stars had. Whatever, *Hong Kong* closed out the series with a whimper—not a bang. Interestingly enough, though, Hope and Crosby were seriously considering resuscitating the *Road* format at the time of Crosby's 1977 death. The new film would have been called, *The Road To Tomorrow*.

Hong Kong, which is strangely lackluster in comparison to the rest of the series, features Hope (fifty-nine years old at the time) as a man on the run from a group of bad guys who want the precious mathematical formula he has managed to memorize and (unbeknownst to them) to forget. Peter Sellers, Zsa Zsa Gabor, Jerry Colonna, Dean Martin, Frank Sinatra and David Niven were among the guest stars who took the last road trip with Crosby and Hope.

The stars of those remarkable seven films have always recalled with fondness the sense of spontaneity and fun that permeated the sets. Hope told one writer that the films were a constant creative "challenge" because he and Crosby were always driven to add just the right bit of schtick or just the right ad libs to the script they had been presented.

"Bing had a writer, Barney Dean, and I had a guy named Monty Brice, who was a great gag man from the Mack Sennett days. . . . He would come up with lines for me to say. And then Bing would come in with something and they'd throw lines and then the surprised look on our faces . . . 'Hey, where'd that come from?' . . . which is the greatest thing in the world because it's so natural."

Hope, like all fans of the *Road* series, marvels over the magic chemistry he and Crosby could create—a "mesh" where the two could play off of one another with little or no rehearsal.

Numerically speaking, of course, the *Road* series was but one small part of Hope's film career. Be-tween the *Road* movies he was still turning out successful movies of his own, movies like:

The Ghostbreakers (1940)—This movie was a remake of a remake. The 1922 version was a remake of a version that had come seven years before with H. B. Warner. In *Ghostbreakers,* Hope was a young reporter gagging his way through misadventures in a haunted castle. Paulette Goddard is Hope's leading lady here. He spends a lot of time scrambling to escape the usual assortment of supernatural menaces. Audiences and critics alike had glowing praise for the film;

Caught In The Draft (1941)—The title is a punny one. The draft Hope has been caught in is strictly military. As film star Don Bolton, Hope teamed with Irving Bacon, Eddie Bracken, Dorothy Lamour, Clarence Kolb and others;

Nothing But The Truth (1941)—This film found Hope as stockbroker Steve Bennett. This time, the gags spring from a bet Hope's character has made $10 thousand to be exact—money Bennett will lose if he's caught telling a lie;

Louisiana Purchase (1941)—One of the kindest things said about this Hope comedy was that it was "undistinguished." As attorney Jim Taylor, Hope played a figure in a Senate investigation.

My Favorite Blonde (1942)—Although less honored and not as well known as the *Road* series, the *My Favorite . . .* series had moments of its own. This film was the first in the three-picture series, reteaming Hope with *Road* writers Don Hartman and Frank Butler.

Blonde is a spy farce, with Hope as a vaudeville performer named Larry Haines. Hope is especially fond of this film because, he says, it allows him to stretch and explore as a comedian. "I wasn't limited," he said, "to slapstick and double takes. This picture spread its humor nicely. Some scripts have big comedy scenes at the start, then the pace dips for about forty minutes and there's another big laugh routine at the end. For my money, a comedy should build up like a snowball, instead of sagging in the middle like an aging mattress."

Blonde found Hope in fine form, out-running the bad guys and, when that fails, trying to dazzle them with blinding wit. One of the film's best-remembered scenes comes when Hope tells his would-be assailant that his knife is showing.

Most of the rest of the film is vintage Hope as well, rife with gags about his alleged penny-pinching ways, his ego and his cowardliness. Paramount was inspired to extend the concept. That extension paved the way to *My Favorite Brunette* in 1947.

Like the other two films in this series, *Brunette* was a spy comedy, setting Hope up once again as the would-be hero caught up in events that are too big—and too dangerous—for him to handle. Dorothy Lamour was the love interest.

Some critics have maintained that *Brunette* is the weakest entry in the *My Favorite . . .* series, but even those cynics have had nothing but praise for the chemistry between Hope and Lamour. Perhaps in part because of the absence of the hugely talented Crosby, Lamour managed to prove herself a comedic actress of no small ability.

Critics and public alike took note and made *Brunette* a hit. Although Hope was as far as ever from his cherished dream of one day walking off with an Oscar, he did receive some of the best notices of his career. In particular, the *Herald Tribune* called Hope's work "brilliant," called Hope himself a "comedian of great stature" and labeled the movie "high artistry."

Among those helping Hope to create that artistry were Lon Chaney, Jr., John Hoyt, Peter Lorre, Willard Robertson, Frank Puglia, Ann Doran and, in a quick cameo appearance, Hope's old road-mate, Crosby.

In this movie Hope once again found himself unwittingly drawn into the detective business. He played a baby photographer who stumbles upon a uranium conspiracy.

My Favorite Spy (1951)—is the third entry of the "Favorite" series and it featured Hope as a burlesque comic. The plot of *My Favorite Spy* is a little more complicated than the first two in the series. Peanuts White (Hope) is the perfect double of superspy Eric Augustine. He is hired to impersonate Augustine and steal some microfilm of plans for a global pilotless plane.

The lunacy of the entire attempt is quite apparent considering that affable, clumsy Hope had to impersonate a suave, sophisticated Augustine. Of course he is captured and the villains think that they have

stumbled on a potential goldmine of secrets. Hope is given a truth serum and when he begins rambling on about his burlesque career, the heavies know their plan has backfired.

Hedy Lamarr is the lady of the picture and she plays Lily Dalbray, a beautiful, talented spy who has worked with Augustine on several other assignments.

The film is set in Tangier and as can be expected, contained the necessary ingredients to be a Hope picture: a chase scene, a few songs and the usual quips and jokes. One of the most entertaining cracks was a scene where Hope smacks his fear-numbed arms and demands: "Get in there, blood." *My Favorite Spy* was as funny as the first "Favorite."

Star Spangled Rhythm (1942)—was done next. Hope had only a guest spot playing himself as a show business emcee. The cast read like a Who's Who, featuring Eddie Bracken, Walter Catlett, Bing Crosby, Cecil B. DeMille, Paulette Goddard, Betty Hutton, Susan Hayward, Alan Ladd, Veronica Lake and Dorothy Lamour.

They Got Me Covered (1943)—featured Bob in one of the typical film vehicles he seemed to prefer. It was a spy comedy which critics called mediocre. The cast included John Abbott, Philip Ahn, Florence Bates, Walter Catlett, Eduardo Ciannelli, Dorothy Lamour, Marion Martin, Donald Meek, Otto Preminger and Mary Treen. It was written by Harry Kurnitz and directed by David Butler, one of Hope's favorites.

Let's Face It (1943)—was another of the typical Hope roles. In this film, an army comedy, he plays Jerry Walker and works with Eve Arden, Dona Drake, Betty Hutton, Arthur Loft, Zasu Pitts, Phyllis Povah, Joseph Sawyer, Raymond Walburn, Marjorie Weaver and Dave Willock. This aPramount production was written by Harry Tugend and directed by Sidney Lanfield.

The Princess and the Pirate (1949)—co-starred Virginia Mayo and gave Hope the chance to indulge in his love of costume dressing. It was a period film and featured the comedian as Sylvester the Great, a trick entertainer. It was another Goldwyn-RKO product and was written by Everett Freeman and two Hope regulars—Don Hartman and Melville Shavelson. The cast also included Walter Brennan and a cameo appearance by Bing Crosby.

Both the *Princess and the Pirate* and the next costume movie Hope did were virtually ignored by critics.

Monsieur Beaucaire (1946)—In this Paramount production Melvin Frank and Norman Panama, two of Hope's gag writers, teamed up to write the script. The comedian plays, the Barber of Madrid, Valentino's old role, dressed in full wig and ruffle regalia. Also included in this film are Hillary Brooke, Joan Caulfield, Constance Collier, Douglas Dumbrille, Cecil Kellaway, Patric Knowles, Mary Nash, Reginald Owen, Marjorie Reynolds and Joseph Schildkraut. It was directed by George Marshall.

The two films Hope made in 1945, before *Monsieur Beaucaire,* have basically been ignored and in some cases forgotten when his complete movies are listed.

All Star Bond Rally (1945)—was a filmed variety show and featured Hope singing the song "Buy, Buy Bonds." It was a Fox Studio release.

Hollywood Victory Caravan (1945) was done by Paramount.

Road to Utopia came next, followed by *Monsieur Beaucaire* and *My Favorite Brunette.*

Where There's Life (1947)—cast Hope in the unusual role of disc jockey Mike Valentine. He was left the keys to a European kingdom to which he was the apparent heir. Unfortunately the inheritance also included a gang of political enemies who paid Hope a "friendly" visit in New York. This movie also featured John Alexander, William Bendix, George Coulouris, Signe Hasso, Dennis Hoey, Joseph Vitale, Harry Von Zell, and George Zucco.

In *Variety Girl* (1947)—Bob had a cameo part playing himself in a variety show along with Mary Hatcher, De Forest Kelley, Torben Meyer, Veronica Lake, Dorothy Lamour, Ray Milland, Alan Ladd, Bing Crosby, Burt Lancaster and a host of others.

Paleface (1948)—was Hope's biggest commercial success without Crosby. It grossed about $4.5 million and made him a top box-office attraction. His salary for one picture by then was $150,000. In this picture, Hope (dentist Painless Peter Potter) weds Calamity Jane (Jane Russell). Unlike many of

his others, *Paleface* did not feature Hope telling nonstop gags. Instead writers Edmund Hartman and Jack Tashlin (with lines added by Jack Rose) wove his jokes in between all the typical Hollywood western features. These included Indians on the war path which was played out in a hilarious capture scene. Hope is tied to a pair of bent trees, one leg to each about to be ripped in two, but he can't resist assuring one of his captors: "You'll get your half."

A saloon scene was also included but, with the modified Bob Hope twist. When he goes through the swinging doors of the saloon they knock him off balance and things just went down hill from there. He was bested by a mug of beer and then found himself in the precarious position of having to demonstrate his courage (an important characteristic in Hollywood westerns). He was forced to take four fingers of rye and typical Hope, he tells the bar keeper to "add the thumb for good measure."

After chuga-lugging the rye, he goes back for more: "Got nothing stronger, huh?" But that was before the rye got to him. When it did, his eyes bugged out, he goes into convulsions and his tough guy personal slithers out the back door chased away by all the laughter.

In this scene he displays what one critic calls "a wonderfully mobile face: eyes capable of widening to alarming proportions, when full knowledge of some imminent danger sinks in and lips which practically curl around his sloped nose in a sneer of contempt or mock ferocity."

His co-star Jane Russell is an interesting change from Lamour. She's the ideal western woman—a sturdy, luscious piece whose very presence played havoc with Hope's blood pressure.

In addition to Russell, this western spoof utilized the talents of Stanley Adams, Iris Adrian, Robert Armstrong, Clem Bevans, Iron Eyes Cody, Jack Searle, Charles Trowbridge, Joseph Vitale, Robert Watson and Jeff York. It was directed by Norman Z. McLeod.

Even though *Paleface* was a smash at the box office the critics' opinions were divided. Bosley Crowther of *The New York Times* described it as "just another amusing run-through of well-worn

slapstick routines by a boy who has bunions on his bunions from the number of times he's run the course." In contrast, Howard Barnes of the *Tribune* wrote: "rarely has he been so funny."

Hope preferred *Paleface* to a subsequent sequel, because it was the original and had the song "Button and Bows" in it. This is the film's featured song which Hope sings, while playing the concertina. In fact, he liked the song so much that he also added it to his stage repertoire, in addition to "Thanks for the Memory" and "It's De-Lovely."

The song was later recorded by Dinah Shore and became a hit, holding the number one spot on the pop charts for over six month.

Paleface was so successful that it spawned the inevitable Paramount follow-up—*Son of Paleface.*

In *Son of Paleface* (1952)—Hope played a Harvard man—Junior—who goes back West to Sawbuck Pass to claim the fortune he thinks his father has hidden. Jane Russell again co-starred with Hope. She plays the part of Mike, whose alias as a saloon singer hid her real identity as the Torch, a female bandit.

When Hope hits town, the two get tangled up romantically and together they escape disasters with the timely aid of Roy Rogers and his faithful horse, Trigger. This duo is also drawn into the western caricature. Rogers showily leaps aboard a speeding stage coach and even Trigger gets into the swing of things when he pulls the covers off Bob in another scene. Of course, no western is complete without a friendly buzzard or two. *Son of Paleface* is no exception. But these are not regular buzzards. They are buzzards Hope-style. They perform.

Roy Rogers and Jane Russell each sang a song and then the three teamed up to sing a jauntier version of "Buttons and Bows"; an acknowledgment, said one critic, that the song deserved better treatment than it received in *Paleface.*

Hope called *Son of Paleface* a nutty picture that people loved. When asked if the hokey directing was what was wrong with the movie, Hope replied: "I wish I had ten more pictures like that, because worldwide that's it. If you can get a picture that satisfies everybody worldwide . . ."

While Hope was pleased with the film, some critics remarked that *Son of Paleface* was just not up to

(left) Road To Morocco" with
Bing Crosby (below) Jane Russell
relaxes on Bobs lap, between
scenes of "Son Of Paleface"

the standards of the original.

In between *Paleface* and its "son," Hope filmed six pictures including the final segment in the "Favorite" trilogy—*My Favorite Spy.*

Sorrowful Jones (1949)—was the first of the six. It was a remake of the Damon Runyon play—*Little Miss Marker.* Co-starring with Lucille Ball, Hope plays a cynical bookie who accidentally becomes guardian of a little girl (Mary Jane Saunders). Hope's decision to be her surrogate father is not altruistic at all. He hopes that doing this good deed will help him during an investigation of his affairs by a racing commission.

Using the girl's name as a cover, Hope and his associates place a large bet on a horse in the big race. Meanwhile, the men who killed the girl's father are after Hope, and all of them are being hunted by a detective.

One writer said: "The film, (*Sorrowful Jones*), makes a half-hearted attempt to remain faithful to one of Runyon's famous and endearing yarns but Hope wavers in his portrayal of the iron-willed Jones. In the scene where the script and the direction have remained true to Runyon's story, Hope is obviously uncomfortable. He appears to be happier tossing off the gags written especially for the remake."

Hope, however, had given Paramount another big box office draw with the help of Bruce Cabot, William Demarest, Thomas Gomez, Paul Lees and Tom Pedi.

When Paramount had a hit in those days it was understood that the formula would be repeated to capture the feeling. One year later it was in:

Fancy Pants (1950)—Keeping Lucille Ball and Bruce Cabot from *Sorrowful Jones,* Hope plays a valet named Humphrey. But again a second wasn't as good as a first. Primarily because *Fancy Pants* was heavy with slapstick and this just wasn't Hope's strong point.

Fancy Pants is set in the west and is based on the novel—*Ruggles of Red Gap,* which was written by Harry Leon Wilson. Hope's adaptation was the fourth remake. The first was made in 1918 by a company called Assanay, starring Taylor Holmes. In 1923 Paramount remade it with Edward Everett Horton playing the lead and then did it again in

1935, this time giving Charles Laughton the top honors.

In between *Sorrowful Jones* and *Fancy Pants,* Paramount inserted:

The Great Lover (1949) another little-discussed film. This movie is number thirty-nine on Hope's film credits and features him as a boy scout leader aboard a ship with a killer (Roland Young) and a mysterious redhead (Rhonda Fleming). It was written by some Hope regulars: Edmund Beloin, Jack Rose and Melville Shavelson and directed by Alexander Hall. Other members of the cast included Sig Arno, Jim Backus, Roland Culver, Jackie Jackson, Jerry Hunter, Richard Lyon, George Reeves and Earl Wright.

After *Fancy Pants,* Hope got another opportunity to play in a Damon Runyon story but:

The Lemon Drop Kid (1951)—didn't fare any better than *Sorrowful Jones.* One reviewer said: ". . . Hope is forced to abandon his comic role and join Marilyn Maxwell (his girlfriend) in song. That one of the songs happens to be "Silver Bells," which is easy enough to take, does not alter the fact that the comedy grinds to a halt while Hope slips disconcertingly into a 'pleasing presence.' "

In this film Hope played the Lemon Drop Kid, a hanger-on in the winner's circle at the track. After he gave racketeer Moose Moran a bad tip which cost $10,000, the comedian spent the rest of the movie trying to raise the replacement cash.

In addition to doing several songs with Maxwell, Hope also had another chance to dress up—this time as Santa Claus and a sixty-year-old doll.

In his next film done for Paramount, Hope appeared as a member of the circus audience in an unbilled crowd scene in *The Greatest Show on Earth* (1952);

Next came *Son of Paleface* and the *Road to Bali;*

Off Limits (1953)—a Paramount production, which is also called 'Military Policemen' features Hope portraying a military cop and the boxing trainer of G.I. Mickey Rooney. It was a comedy which once more found Hope at sea. This time however, his stomach couldn't take it and he goes for the jar of smelling salts. It turned out to be a jar of peanut butter. The high point of the film saw Hope deliberately wreck a car he thought belonged to a mortal enemy. When he found that the car actually belonged to his superior, Hope knew he was done for and he croaks whisperingly: "Just a quiet funeral, sir."

The cast included Stanley Clements, Carolyn Jones, Marilyn Maxwell, Eddie Mayehoff, Marvin Miller and John Ridgely. The film was directed by one of Hope's favorites—George Marshall.

"I wish he were alive," said Hope in one interview. "God he was marvelous. He had a lot of stuff up there," he said pointing to his head. "He directed two reelers, when he started, like Leo McCarey; and he had this tremendous store of comedy bits that he'd think of us as he'd go along . . ."

In *Here Come the Girls* (1953)—Hope play'd Stanley Snodgrass, a chorus boy grown older. One critic said: "In spite of dull sub-Ziegfield musical numbers, *Here Come the Girls* enshrines one of Hope's most fastidiously timed, delicately posturing, visually and vocally subtle incarnations of camp comic complacency. Other cast members in this film included Fred Clark, Rosemary Clooney, Arlene Dahl, William Demarest, Tony Martin, Mildred Mitchell and Robert Strauss. It was written by Edmund Hartmann and Hal Kanter and directed by Claude Binyon.

Scared Stiff (1953)—features Hope in a cameo role in a film he had once had the lead in—*Ghostbreakers*. This film features another popular and successful movie duo—Dean Martin and Jerry Lewis.

Casanovas's Big Night (1954)—was another period piece and one of the last films done under Hope's Paramount contract. Joan Fontaine co-stars with Hope, who plays a tailor's apprentice; a highly unusual role for our usually clumsy hero, especially with a name like Pippo Poppolino. Set in Venice, Italy, *Casanova* is the last period piece the comedian did. He plays an apprentice who masquerades as the Great Lover. He is hired by a rich duchess to test the virtue of her prospective daughter-in-law. The entire film hangs on the ability of Hope to perpetuate his farcial identity. But it seems that Hope's days as a one-man cavalry to the rescue are over. Like the rest of his costume films, *Casanova* doesn't come up to scratch.

Other cast members included John Carradine,

Audrey Dalton, Hope Emerson, Arnold Moss and Basil Rathbone. It was directed by Norman Z. McLeod and written by Edmund Hartmann and Hal Kanter.

Hope's next film is an abrupt and rather radical departure from what his audiences have come to expect.

The Seven Little Foys (1955)—was released by Paramount. It was a film biography of Eddie Foy, Sr. and his family of vaudeville performers. One critic speculated that this fact—the vaudeville connection—must have played a big part in Hope's decision to take the role. It was his first film attempt at serious comedy and the desire to tackle this type of script was probably the result of the repeated questions about his acting ability.

The film was a joint venture between Scribe Productions—an independent company owned by screen writers Jack Rose and Mel Shavelson (gagmen from Hope's radio days), Paramount and Hope Enterprises. The fact that the comedian actually put some of his own money into the project is probably a very good indication of its importance to him.

Every precaution was taken to ensure its success. The script was tailored to Hope's unique talent; Eddie Foy, Jr. was consulted and used as narrator and Hope practiced his dance numbers for a month with Nick Castle before shooting even began.

The film dealt with Eddie Foy's decision to launch a vaudeville team made up of himself and his seven children; a decision he made, said one of his sons, because he wanted to keep as many children as he could between himself and the audience.

Because the film was about vaudeville, the dancing and singing had to be of the quality done in these shows and Hope was delighted to find that for all his years away from his first show business arena, he hadn't lost the touch.

When he played the part of Foy, Hope could not gloss it over and fudge around the edges. He had to get down to some serious comedy acting, because Foy was definitely not an angel temporarily pulled from the path of good. He was a totally selfish man, no matter what the situation. In one scene, for example, Hope (as Foy) enjoys himself drinking at the Friars Club while his wife lay dying in the hospital a few blocks away.

(inset above) "Paris Holiday" with Fernandel (inset below) "Off Limits" with Marilyn Maxwell and Mickey Rooney. (left) Another scene from "They Got Me Covered"

Although *The Seven Little Foys* was a serious comedy, it did include a number of Hope-type gags, but not enough, felt one critic, to soften the calculating side of Foy.

While this criticism might have been valid if Hope was trying to do a typical Hope comedy, it was, in this instance, more a case of nostalgia interfering with the viewing of reality. Kind of like parents unwilling to let their child grow up.

Other critics rejoiced, making sly digs at Crosby, saying that Hope wouldn't have to take any more insults from his "Road" pal and could stand with pride among the serious actors in Hollywood.

The movie was directed by Melville Shavelson, who also did the writing in conjunction with Jack Rose.

After the *Foy* film, Hope continued to flex his serious acting reflexes:

That Certain Feeling (1956)—is one of the most sophisticated and polished Hope films. He plays Francis Y. Digman, a gifted but neurotic cartoonist who is unable to keep his job or his wife (Eva Marie Saint). The movie was based on the Broadway play—*King of Hearts*—written by Jean Kerr and Eleanor Brooke.

In *That Certain Feeling* Hope is forced to exercise considerable restraint on his tendency to play "top-that-gag." He's able to do this, proving to himself and others that this vaudeville stand-up comedian did know how to handle more subtle comedy.

All this doesn't mean there weren't any funny lines in the film. There were, but they were worked skillfully into the story line. In one scene for instance, Eva hands him the morning paper and he comments: "Not the first thing I reach for in the morning as you doubtless recall." His suave rival, George Sanders, is not immune from Hope quips. When he saw his penthouse he remarked: "That's what I like—everything done in contrasting shades of money."

In *Iron Petticoat* (1956)—Hope goes in the exact opposite direction—totally no self-control; like the orgy after a fast. This film was originally conceived as a Ninotchka-type farce, but even with

91

co-star Katherine Hepburn, the film disintegrated into a vehicle for Bob Hope gags.

Ben Hecht, a top-flight writer who did the script was so incensed by the treatment of his script that he took out a $275 ad on the back of the *Hollywood Reporter* which said:

My Dear Partner Bob Hope:

This is to notify you that I have removed my name as author from our mutilated venture, *The Iron Petticoat.*

Unfortunately, your other partner, Katherine Hepburn, can't shy out of the fractured picture with me.

Although her magnificent comic performance has been blow-torched out of the film, there is enough left of the Hepburn footage to identify her for her sharpshooters.

I am assured by my hopeful predators that the *Iron Petticoat* will go over big with people "who can't get enough of Bob Hope."

Let us hope this swooning contingent is not confined to yourself and your euphoric agent, Louis Shurr.

(Signed) Ben Hecht

Hope retaliated with a letter on the same page in the next issue of the *Reporter.* He implied that since Hecht had left the film, it had improved. He signed his retort: Bob (Blow Torch) Hope.

After all these public shenanigans, Hope went back to work and released another film.

Beau James (1957)—found the comedian again switching directions, this time back toward a serious vein. Released by Paramount, *Beau James,* like *Foy,* was based on fact. Hope played Jimmy Walker, an eastside kid who became one of New York City's most flamboyant mayors. The script was based on the biography of Walker called *Beau James* which was written by newspaperman Gene Fowler, a Walker intimate.

Resisting the easy route—another joke-laden *tour de force,* the two writers produced a perceptive character study. Walker was a charming rogue, whose vices were explicitly detailed on screen. And Hope faced a major challenge: portraying a character who was a true philanderer instead of a make-believe one. He also had to project a believable image of a man who thought being mayor was a

way to get unlimited access to New York high life. Walker's indifference toward his municipal responsibilities led to the Seabury probe. This massive investigation uncovered a seething ocean of corruption.

One critic put it this way: "One of the film's principal assets is its adroit use of humor to depict Walker's complex personality. After all, he was not a hack. He was a rogue, a slicker who knew at all times exactly what he was."

Hope emerged in *Beau James* as an actor of surprising talent, slipping completely into his character as if it were a cocoon. Late in the film, a broke and broken Walker is forced to hustle up some money to buy a steamship ticket into exile. Hope brings touching poignancy to his portrayal of the beaten man leaving the city he loves. Walker is no saint, and the audience knows that; still, Hope imbues the part with such feeling that it's hard not to be sympathetic, even armed with the knowledge that the character is only getting what he deserves.

Of course, Hope being Hope, the film also has its comedic flourishes. There is, for instance, the line in which a well-wisher greets him as "Mr. Mayor." Hope, mindful of the snickers with which his candidacy has been greeted, is wittily self-effacing: "Smile when you say that," he retorts. "Everybody else does."

The uneasy strain between comedy and drama was picked up on by some of the critics and the general consensus among that group was that Paramount was uncomfortable with the idea of the beloved comic playing a bad guy. *Beau James* also failed, in the eyes of some critics, to deal with the possibility that the real Walker might have been guilty as charged of the sins that drove him into his exile. Hope's *Beau James* guest stars included Darren McGavin, Vera Miles and Jimmy Durante, who played himself.

Paris Holiday (1958)—As the title implies, this comedy concerns a French vacation. Hope is a movie star. Anita Ekberg, Preston Sturges, Fernandel and Alan Gifford are all among the co-stars.

Showdown at Ulcer Gulch (1958)—Hope teamed up with Edie Adams, Orson Bean, Ernie Kovacs and Marx Brothers Groucho and Chico to make this promotional film for *The Saturday Evening Post.*

Five Pennies (1959)—Hope played Hope, turning in a cameo appearance in this story of jazzman Red Nichols.

Alias Jesse James (1959)—Even the premise sounds funny. Hope is Milford Farnsworth, life insurance salesman in the Old West. His predictable misadventures team him with such western heroes as Roy Rogers, Gary Cooper, James Arness and Fess Parker. In addition, Bing Crosby, the Crooner himself, turns in a guest appearance.

Facts of Life (1960)—Hope and Lucille Ball team up as a couple married—but not to each other. Their decision to have an affair leads to tender comedy. Longtime Hope gagman Melvin Frank directed the film from a script he co-wrote with Norman Panama. Hope's co-stars included Mike Mazurki, Louis Nye, Louise Beavers, Don DeFore, Marianne Stewart and Peter Leeds.

Bachelor in Paradise (1961)—Hope and Lana Turner find themselves in a box-office smash. Co-stars included Jim Hutton, Janis Paige, Don Porter, John McGiver, Paula Prentiss, Virginia Grey and Clinton Sundberg.

Critic's Choice (1963)—Hope and Lucille Ball are a battling husband and wife. The bone of contention is Ball's writing career, which is constantly belittled and ridiculed by her snide spouse. *Choice* was an attempt to bring to the screen what had been a popular stage comedy by Ira Levin. That version had starred Henry Fonda.

Hope and Ball are teamed with Rip Torn, Jim Backus, Marilyn Maxwell, Lurene Tuttle, Jessie Royce Landis, Jerome Cowan, Stanley Adams, Marie Windsor and Rick Kellman. The film is widely considered to be just another in a largely uninterrupted run of mediocre films with which Hope capped his career on the big screen.

Call Me Bwana (1963)—Hope is a writer on safari in Africa, joined by Anita Ekberg, Edie Adams, Lionel Jeffries and Percy Herbert.

The Sound of Laughter (1963)—This was a documentary on early film comedy. Hope was spotlighted in a clip from *Going Spanish,* singing a duet with Leah Ray.

A Global Affair (1964)—Sixty-one-year-old Hope attempts to pass himself off as a swinging bachelor surrounded by a bevy of beautiful girls.

"Cancel My Reservation" with Eve Marie Saint.

He'd have probably been just as convincing playing an eight-year-old boy. Although Hope has always looked younger as his age advanced past the fifty mark, the fact is that he's not a young man and *Affair* pointed that out in no uncertain terms.

Elga Andersen, Michele Mercier and Lilo Pulver are among the performers trapped in this movie with Hope.

I'll Take Sweden (1965)—Frankie Avalon, Tuesday Weld and Dina Merrill join Hope in a domestic comedy set in Sweden as his critical fortunes continue to slide.

Boy, Did I Get a Wrong Number (1966)—Hope is a husband caught up in a rather compromising situation with Elke Sommer, who plays one scene wearing a towel and nothing else. Phyllis Diller played Hope's irrreverent maid. Although the film did fairly well in the United States, British audiences were unimpressed with it.

Benny Baker, Cesare Danova, Joyce Jameson, Marjorie Lord and Harry Von Zell are among

Hope's co-stars.

Eight on the Lam (1967)—The swinging, would-be ladies' man finds himself a family man in this one—a widower, to be exact, saddled with seven children. As the title implies, dad and the kids are on the run. Phyllis Diller, Kevin Brody, Shirley Eaton and Jill St. John all co-starred. Two of Hope's grandkids, Avis and Robert Hope were among his "children" in the movie.

The Private Navy of Sgt. O'Farrell (1968)—World War II schtick, co-starring Gina Lollobrigida, William Wellman, Jr., Phyllis Diller and Henry Wilcoxon.

How to Commit Marriage (1969)—That then-hot topic, the generation gap, came in for some ribbing in this film, co-starring Irwin Corey, Jackie Gleason, Tina Louise, Leslie Nielsen, Maureen Arthur, Paul Stewart and Jane Wyman.

Cancel My Reservation (1972)—Hope's last movie was the first movie ever to premiere at New York City's Radio Music Hall, but that bit of history didn't stop the critics from ripping it up. The sixty-nine-year-old comic was cast as a talk-show host suspected of murder. As if that's not bad enough, Hope also has to contend with Eva Marie Saint, who plays his wife in a marriage on the skids. Bing Crosby, Flip Wilson, John Wayne and Johnny Carson all put in cameo appearances.

To sum up, then, Bob Hope's films have firmly established him in the minds of his fans and late-movie trivia buffs, as the same brash cowardly character of television and radio fame. But some critics have noted with apparent amazement the fact that Hope was a more than competent serious actor.

Of course, he never got to display that side in most of the comedies the studios were dreaming up for him; the fact is, Hope had an actor's natural ability to lose himself inside a character, to zip it up around him as if it were a sleeping bag. It was that ability, as much or more than anything else, that gave him his durability in films. It was also that ability that allowed him to make the seemingly simpler slapstick comedy routines work. As any comic would surely attest, the art of making people laugh is three times as difficult as it seems, and if a person is able to overcome that and make the whole thing *look* easy, then that person is a performer of awe-inspiring talent.

Unfortunately, that very talent has often caused Hope to be overlooked and underrated when critics get together to pontificate. The problem seems to be that he makes it all look *too* easy, so that he's tossed off time and time again by so-called "serious" movie people as just a transplated comedian with a pleasing delivery.

One critic said that the reason other film critics failed to take Hope's work seriously is that he failed to create a larger-than-life comic persona, à la Mae West (the sultry sex goddess), W. C. Fields (the eternally inebriated, eternally cynical hater of children and dogs), or the Marx Brothers (the wackos). That's an arguable point, at best. As another writer noted, Hope's screen persona is quintessentially American—perhaps more so than Fields, West, and the Marxes. He was the breezy, easygoing Anyman, the fellow who only asks of life that it keep him reasonably warm, reasonably satiated where his physical and mental needs are concerned, and reasonably amused.

Anyman is not a muscle-bound brute. Rather, he is the long-suffering *victim* of the muscle-bound brute, the fellow, who, in the face of bullying, comes precariously close to caving in before tapping into his hidden storehouse of courage to give the brute the whipping he deserves. He is funny when he's cowardly, inspiring when he is brave.

Hope amplified on all those themes in the bulk of his films. His cowardly chumps were the guy next door, or the guy down the street, who's been kicked in the chops often by life, but always manages to answer the bell one more time. In that, his comic persona was more human and more down-to-earth than those of most of the actors with whom he is often compared.

When he talked back to the bad guys and, miraculously, found the strength of character to back up his talk, Hope was striking for millions of so-called "little guys" out there. And they appreciated him for it.

Hope often complains with a certain wistfulness in his voice that it would have been nice to have won an Oscar for his acting. But in the final analysis, any self-respecting film buff must wonder if that oversight is really Hope's loss—or Hollywood's?

THE LEGEND

IT DOESN'T SEEM LIKE it, it's hard to conceive and it's revoltingly depressing to even consider it, but one day we won't have Bob Hope to kick us around any more. And on that day we'll hear eulogies and read tributes and watch mourners, with a certain numbness clouding our perspective.

It's difficult, of course, to imagine a world without Bob Hope. Like baseball, Mt. Rushmore and the Statue of Liberty, he's been around so long it's like he's always been around and always will be—an unchanging part of the ever-changing American landscape.

But baseball is a game, Rushmore is a mountain and Lady Liberty a statue. Bob Hope, for all his radiant good health and his adherence to a schedule that would demolish someone half his age, is just a man. His durability, his amazing record, the miles he's traveled, the films he's made, the shows he's given . . . all of these sometimes tend to obscure that fact. He's a legend, sure. But even legends are just women and men.

On the day the laughter stops, there'll be weeping and crying but let's hope not too much. We hope the memory of the laughter will comfort and soothe.

And for now, we don't even need memory. The laughter lives—louder than ever. Let's enjoy it.

95

OTHER STARBOOKS

REACH OUT (ISBN #0-89531-036-8)
The Diana Ross story   Leonard Pitts Jr
PAPA JOE'S BOYS (ISBN #0-89531-037-6)
The Jacksons story   Leonard Pitts Jr
HOLLYWOOD HUNKS (ISBN #0-89531-034-1)
                                        Jacquelyn Nicholson
MUSICMANIA (ISBN #0-89531-038-4)   Robyn Flans
MR WONDERFUL (ISBN #0-89531-078-3)
The Stevie Wonder story   Leonard Pitts Jr
JUDY LIZA (ISBN #0-89531-079-1)   **Michael S. Barson**
THE GLAMOUR GIRLS OF HOLLYWOOD
(ISBN #0-89531-079-1)   Leonard Pitts Jr

For purchase of any of the above titles, send $5.95 plus $1.00 postage
and handling to: Sharon's Sales Dept., 105 Union Ave., Cresskill, N.J.
07626